D1789677

American-Swedish Handbook

13th edition

Editor
Holly Johnson, SCA Projects Manager

Layout Editor
Tom Lewis

Compiled by
Elise Peters, SCA Director of Affiliates
Jamie Olson

Proofreaders
Glen Brolander, Laurie Dahlberg Fulton,
Anne-Charlotte Harvey, Barbro Lundberg,
Mark Magnusson

© Swedish Council of America, 2004

ISBN 0-9609620-7-7

Swedish Council of America
2600 Park Avenue
Minneapolis, MN 55407

Phone: 612.871.0593
Fax: 612.871.0687

Printed in the United States of America.

Sexton Printing, Inc.
250 East Lothenbach Avenue
St. Paul, MN 55118

Contents

Letter from the SCA Chairman

The 13th edition of the *American-Swedish Handbook* is a publication of the Swedish Council of America. It contains listings of nearly 1,000 Swedish-American and Scandinavian-American organizations and offices including: Embassies and Consulates, organizations in the United States, Canada, and Sweden, national organizations, educational organizations and publications. New sections in this edition feature the organizations in Canada as well as the national organizations. We are proud to highlight our 340 affiliated organizations throughout this edition.

Celebrating the fifth edition produced by the Council and the 25th anniversary of this resource, it is our hope that this 13th edition will prove to be a valuable resource for all persons interested in Swedish-North American relations and in the Swedish heritage in the United States and Canada. The *American-Swedish Handbook* publication was instituted in 1943 as a project of The Augustana Swedish Institute, Rock Island, IL. Eight editions were published by this organization. When the Institute discontinued as a separate organization, the project was transferred to the Swedish Council of America.

The Council is grateful to the Barbro Osher Pro Suecia Foundation for its generous gift in supporting the *Handbook*'s publication. We also thank the Embassy of Sweden for its financial support. The current volume has been the responsibility of the Council's Projects Manager, Holly Johnson. Supporting work has been done by SCA's Director of Affiliates, Elise Peters and SCA Intern, Jamie Olson. The Council deeply appreciates their work as well as the work completed by numerous proof-readers. The Council also expresses thanks to all information contributors. It is due to this cooperation that this volume exists.

We are confident that this 13th edition of the *American-Swedish Handbook* will continue to preserve the Swedish heritage in North America and continue to foster relationships between the United States, Canada, and Sweden.

Rev. Paul M. Cornell, Chair
Swedish Council of America

Introduction:
The Swedish Council of America

The Swedish Council of America is an international umbrella organization, representing over 300 associations, organizations and groups—and over 70,000 individual members—who share a passion for preserving the Swedish heritage and sharing ties, both old and new, between Sweden and North America. For over 30 years, the Council has worked to promote the understanding of Swedish culture and heritage in the "New World."

Founded in 1972, the SCA has gathered over 300 Swedish-American organizations throughout the United States and Canada under its umbrella, representing interests ranging from Swedish immigration history and preservation to Swedish choral music, from folk dancing to international business. The Council counts among its affiliates Swedish-American lodges and fraternal organizations, colleges, museums, consulates, chambers of commerce, historical societies, women's groups, businesses, churches, music and dance groups, and many other organizations—all dedicated to promoting Swedish heritage. The government of Sweden is also supportive of the SCA's operations: the Swedish Ambassador to the U.S. often attends the Council's events; his involvement underscores the strong ties the SCA enjoys with the government and embassy of Sweden.

The mission of the Swedish Council of America is to bring into a cooperative relationship all groups and individuals whose purpose is to promote knowledge and understanding of the Swedish heritage in American life and to strengthen the cultural ties between North America and Sweden. It is the vision of the Council to be the pre-eminent organization that exists to assist affiliated organizations in preserving and enriching the Swedish heritage in North America through programs, funding, communication and activities in partnership with all Swedish

Americans promoting a continued strong relationship between
North America and Sweden.

The Swedish Council of America plays a vital role in preserving Swedish-American heritage throughout North America, and
in promoting knowledge and appreciation of Swedish culture by:

• Serving as the leading source for information about Sweden
  and Swedish-American topics and events

• Offering practical assistance to individuals and organizations
  through direct access to the SCA via its website and offices in
  Minneapolis and Sweden

• Publishing the informative SCA *Update* (in print and
  online), as well publishing the *American-Swedish Handbook*,
  the only comprehensive sourcebook for all Swedish-
  American organizations in North America

• Providing financial grants to support significant Swedish-
  American projects

• Honoring the work and commitment of individuals on the
  local or regional level through the Award of Merit

• Recognizing outstanding Americans and Swedes for their
  important contributions to humanity through the Great
  Swedish Heritage Awards and America's Swede of the Year
  Awards

• Exemplifying excellence by providing a young scientist the
  opportunity to participate in the Nobel ceremonies in
  Sweden through the Council's Glenn T. Seaborg Science
  Award

• Engaging new generations in learning about Sweden and
  Swedish America through the SCA's biennial Conference of
  Swedish America

- Promoting wider knowledge of Swedish heritage and contemporary Sweden through support of the popular quarterly magazine, *Nordic Reach*, and especially its "Sweden & America" section and identity.

The Swedish Council of America is governed by a board of directors and maintains offices and staff in Minneapolis. It is chartered in Minnesota as a nonprofit corporation under Section 501 (c)(3) of the Internal Revenue Code. For more information about the Council, please visit our website *www.swedishcouncil.org*.

Officers & Directors of the Swedish Council of America

OFFICERS

Rev. Paul M. Cornell
Chair
Collegeville, PA

Dr. Patricia McFate
Vice Chair;
Chair, Grants
Santa Fe, NM

Bruce R. Larson
Secretary
Rochester, MN

Robert A. Peterson
Treasurer; Chair, Finance
Tucson, AZ

Donald E. Benson
Chair, Governance &
Nominating
Minneapolis, MN

Siri M. Eliason
Chair, Royal Round Table;
Co-Chair, Sweden Office
San Francisco, CA

E. Jan Hartmann
Immediate Past Chair; Chair,
Internal Communications
Naples, FL

Dr. Nils Hasselmo
Chairman Emeritus;
Co-Chair, Futures Committee
Washington, DC

Lennart N. Johansson
Chair, Publications/Editorial
Ann Arbor, MI

Kerstin Lane
Chair, Cultural Affairs
Chicago, IL

Urban Lundberg
Chair, Awards & Recognition
Sterling Heights, MI

Bertil O. Lundh
Co-Chair, Sweden Office;
Co-Chair, Futures Committee
Seattle, WA

11

DIRECTORS

Suzanne K. Ahlstrand
Wichita, KS

Clarence Anderson
Jenison, MI

Dr. Philip Anderson
Chicago, IL

Karl G. Andrén
New York, NY

Steven Bahls
Rock Island, IL

Dr. Dag Blanck
Stockholm, Sweden

Margaret (Sally) Bridwell
Berwyn, PA

Donald Borgeson
Naples, FL

Glen E. Brolander
Chairman Emeritus
Salem, SC

Dr. George Brushaber
St. Paul, MN

Dr. Å.G. Ulf Brynjestad
Alpine, CA

Dennis Carlson
Decatur, GA

Neil Carlson
Winnipeg, Manitoba, Canada

Kim Erickson
Minnetonka, MN

Dr. Paul Formo
Lindsborg, KS

Marianne Forssblad
Seattle, WA

Laurie Dahlberg Fulton
Douglasville, GA

Barbara Carlson Gage
Minnetonka, MN

Henry Gooss
New York, NY

William Gusenius
Lindsborg, KS

Erik Gustavson
Karlstad, Sweden

Willow Hagans
Detroit, MI

Dr. Anne-Charlotte Harvey
Lemon Grove, CA

Jahn R. Hedberg
Seattle, WA

Dr. David Horner
Chicago, IL

Rev. Dennis Johnson
Minneapolis, MN

Ronald J. Johnson
Madison, WI

Herbert Johnson
Marietta, GA

Dr. Theodore Johnson
Duluth, MN

Dr. William Johnson
Three Rivers, MI

Bruce Karstadt
Minneapolis, MN

David Larson
La Quinta, CA

O. Greg Linde
Cloverdale, CA

Dr. Edward Lindell
Edina, MN

Lennart Lindell
Sycamore, IL

Dr. Luther S. Luedtke
Thousand Oaks, CA

Franklin Mead
Boston, MA

Michael L. Miller
Cleveland, OH

David Monson
North Oaks, MN

Agneta Nilsson
Manhattan Beach, CA

Alan J. Olson
Boulder, CO

Gerald Pearson
Okoboji, IA

Dr. James Peterson
St. Peter, MN

L. Durand Peterson
Jamestown, NY

Sandra Pfaff
Haverford, PA

Herbert Rambo
Berlin, NJ

DIRECTORS, *continued*

Annette Seaberg
  Chicago, IL

John Sellstrom
  Jamestown, NY

Ted Simonson
  Winnipeg, Manitoba, Canada

Bengt Sohlén
  Minneapolis, MN

Kerstin Trowbridge
  Grand Rapids, MI

Paul Upcraft
  Edina, MN

Richard Waldron
  Philadelphia, PA

Curt Westrom
  Bemus Point, NY

Dr. Nils William Olson
  Founding Executive Director
  Winter Park, FL

Nils Y. Wessell
  Founding President
  Naples, FL

Ambassador Jan Eliasson
  Honorary Member
  Washington, DC

Affiliate Members

FOUNDING & SUSTAINING MEMBERS
American Swedish Historical Museum, PA
American Swedish Institute, MN
A.U.S.S. Cultural Heritage Foundation, FL
Detroit Swedish Council, MI
Gammelgården Museum, MN
Gustavus Adolphus College, MN
Norden Club of Jamestown, NY
SACC-USA, VA
Swedish American Historical Society, IL

SUPPORTING MEMBERS
Arpi Swedish Male Chorus of Metropolitan Detroit, MI
Augustana Heritage Association, IL
Bethany College, KS
Birger Sandzen Memorial Gallery, KS
Emigrant Institute, Växjö, Sweden
IOV–Ellida Lodge #25, IL
Iowa City Swedish Club, IA
Lakehead Social History Institute, Ontario, Canada
Mt. Jewett Swedish Festival, PA
Nisswa-Stämman, MN
Northwest Iowa Associates of ASF, IA
Scandinavian Library, Inc., MA
Scandinavian Seminar, MA
Silicon Vikings, CA
Sons of Norway, MN
SWEA, Arizona, AZ
Swedish Club of Houston, TX

SUPPORTING MEMBERS, *continued*

Swedish Heritage Society of Utah, UT
The Scandinavians, Inc., CO

ASSOCIATE MEMBERS

Agassiz Swedish Heritage Society, MN
American Daughters of Sweden, IL
American Nyckelharpa Association, PA
American Scandinavian Association of the Great Plains, KS
American Scandinavian Heritage Foundation, NY
American Society of Swedish Engineers, PA
American Union of Swedish Singers, OR
Andrew Inc. of Princeton, MN
ASA at Augustana College, IL
ASF of Thousand Oaks, CA
ASI–Male Chorus, MN
ASI Male Chorus Auxiliary, MN
ASI Spelmanslag, MN
Augustana College, IL
Augustana Historical Society, IL
Austin Scandinavian Club, TX
Bemidji Affiliate of ASI, MN
Bethany College, KS
Bethel University, MN
Bethel Lutheran Church, IL
Bishop Hill Heritage Association, IL
Bridge to Sweden, NY
Cadillac Area Scandinavian Society, MI
California Lutheran University, CA
Carl Sandburg Historic Site Association, IL
Center for Scandinavian Studies, MN
Central Iowa Associates of the American-Scandinavian
    Foundation, IA

Church of Sweden Abroad, CA
City of Lindsborg, KS
Concordia Language Villages, MN
Consulate General of Sweden–Los Angeles, CA
Consulate General of Sweden–New York, NY
Consulate General of Sweden–San Francisco, CA
Consulate of Sweden–Georgia, GA
Consulate of Sweden–Nova Scotia, Canada
Consulate of Sweden–Puerto Rico
Dala Heritage Society, MN
Dalesburg Scandinavian Association, SD
Delaware Swedish Colonial Society, DE
Duluth Sister Cities Commission, MN
Duluth-Vaxjö Soccer Exchange, Inc, MN
Emigrant Register, Karlstad, Sweden
Eriksen Translations Inc, NY
Fairmount Park Art Association, PA
FEST!, MN
Flickorna Fem, MN
Folklife Institute of Kansas, KS
Föreningen Svenskar i Världen, Stockholm, Sweden
Forgat Mig Ej Childrens Club, IL
Fox Valley Swedish Society, WI
Friends of Cordelia Committee, ID
Friends of Scandinavia, NC
Friends of the Swedish Cabin, PA
Genealogical Society of Salem County, NJ
Geneva Chamber of Commerce, IL
Genline–Swedish Church Records Online, IL
Gustavus Adolphus Lutheran Church, NY
Historic Preservation Trust of Berks County, PA
Hostel, Göteborg, Sweden

House of Sweden, CA
Idun Guild, MN
Independent Order of Svithiod, IL
Independent Order of Vikings, IL
Indiana University School of Music, IN
IOS–Brage Lodge #29, IL
IOS–Svithiod Lodge #1, IL
IOV–Ingjald Lodge #65, NY
IOV–Skandia Lodge #68, OR
Isanti County Historical Society, MN
Jacobson House Native Art Center, OK
Jamestown Community College, NY
Jenny Lind Club, MI
John Ericsson Society, NY
Kalmar Nyckel Foundation, DE
Key of See Storytellers, MN
Kichi-Saga Swedish Club, MN
Kingsburg Chamber of Commerce, CA
Kittson County Historical Society, MN
Lake Region Swedish Heritage Society, ND
Leiv Eriksson International Festival, MN
Lindsborg Chamber of Commerce, KS
Lindsborg Swedish Folk Dancers, KS
Linneas of Texas, TX
Lutheran Social Services, NY
Maple Ridge Swedish Study Circle, MN
Minnehaha Academy, MN
Musikförlaget Vallmon, Sunne, Sweden
Neighbors Abroad of Palo Alto, CA
New Sweden Centre, DE
New Sweden Cultural Heritage Society of OR & WA
New Sweden Historical Society, ME

Noon Day Scandinavian Club, NE
Norden Folk, WI
Norden Music International, CA
Norden Women's Club, NY
Nordic Heritage Museum, WA
Nordic Study Circle, WA
Nordiska Museet, Stockholm, Sweden
Nordstjernan-Swedish News, Inc, CT
North Park University: Center for Scandinavian Studies, IL
Norwegian American Foundation, WA
Oakland Chamber of Commerce, NE
Ozark Scandinavian Society of Springfield, Missouri, MO
Positive Sweden/North America, CA
Prairie Public Television, ND
Raoul Wallenberg Committee of the US, NY
Reford Gardens, Quebec, Canada
Rhode Island Swedish Heritage Association, RI
Riksföreningen Sverigekontakt, Göteborg, Sweden
Ryssby Committee, CO
SACC, Atlanta, GA
SACC, Chicago, IL
SACC, Colorado, CO
SACC, Detroit, MI
SACC, Greater Los Angeles, CA
SACC, Minnesota, MN
SACC, San Francisco, CA
SACC, Texas, TX
San Antonio Scandinavians, TX
San Francisco Performances, CA
Scandia Women's Chorus, MI
Scandinavian American Cultural & Historical Foundation, CA
Scandinavian American Foundation of Georgia, GA

Scandinavian American Heritage Society, NJ
Scandinavian Association of Greater Kansas City, KS
Scandinavian Center at Nansen Field, CA
Scandinavian Chamber Orchestra of New York, NY
Scandinavian Club of Columbus, OH
Scandinavian Club of Hot Spring Village, AR
Scandinavian Cultural Center, WA
Scandinavian Cultural Center at CLU, CA
Scandinavian Cultural Center of Santa Cruz, CA
Scandinavian Cultural Society of Greater Hartford, CT
Scandinavian Department, University of Wisconsin, WI
Scandinavian Fest Inc., NJ
Scandinavian Folk Festival, NY
Scandinavian Friends, TX
Scandinavian Heritage Foundation, OR
Scandinavian Heritage Society of Kentucky, KY
Scandinavian Home Society, Ontario, Canada
Scandinavian Old Time Fiddle Society, MN
Scandinavian Program–University of Michigan German
    Department, MI
Scandinavian Society of Wichita, KS
Seattle Chamber Players, WA
Stanton Historical Society, IA
Stockholm Historical Society, ME
Stockholm Institute, WI
Stromsburg Chamber of Commerce, NE
Sveaborg, MD
Svensk Hyllningsfest, KS
Svenska Klubben, WI
Svenska Mammor, NY
Svenska Skolföreningen in Orange County, CA
Svenska Troller, CA

Svenska Vänner, ND
Svenska Vännerna, Inc., MN
Svenskarnas Dag, MN
Svenskarnas Dag Girls Choir, MN
Sverige-Amerika Stiftelsen, Stockholm, Sweden
SWEA International, CA
SWEA, Atlanta, GA
SWEA, Boston, MA
SWEA, Buffalo, NY
SWEA, Chicago, IL
SWEA, Dallas, TX
SWEA, Denver, CO
SWEA, Los Angeles, CA
SWEA, Michigan, MI
SWEA, Minnesota, MN
SWEA, New Jersey, NJ
SWEA, New Orleans, LA
SWEA, New York, CT
SWEA, North Carolina, NC
SWEA, San Diego, CA
SWEA, San Francisco, CA
SWEA, Seattle, WA
SWEA, South Florida, FL
SWEA, Texas, TX
SWEA, Vancouver, British Columbia, Canada
SWEA, Virginia Beach, VA
SWEA, Washington DC
Swedes of the Grand Valley, CO
Swedish American Bicentennial Fellowship Fund, Stockholm,
    Sweden
Swedish American Central Association of Southern
    California, CA

Swedish American Council of Boston, MA
Swedish American Heritage Society of Western Michigan, MI
Swedish American Historical Association of California, CA
Swedish American Historical Society of Wisconsin, WI
Swedish American Museum of Chicago, IL
Swedish American Patriotic League, CA
Swedish American Society of Tidewater, VA
Swedish Club of Denver, CO
Swedish Club of Detroit, MI
Swedish Club of Los Angeles, CA
Swedish Club of San Francisco and the Bay Area, CA
Swedish Club of Sarasota, FL
Swedish Colonial Society, PA
Swedish Consulate of Arizona, AZ
Swedish Council of St. Louis, MO
Swedish Country Interiors, WA
Swedish Cultural Association of Manitoba, Manitoba, Canada
Swedish Cultural Center, Inc., WA
Swedish Cultural Committee, Inc., NE
Swedish Cultural Heritage Society of the Red River Valley, MN
Swedish Cultural Society of Cleveland, OH
Swedish Cultural Society of Duluth, MN
Swedish Cultural Society of Rockford, IL
Swedish Foundation of Iowa's Swede Bend Settlement, MO
Swedish Genealogical Society of Minnesota, MN
Swedish Heritage Society of North Dakota, ND
Swedish Heritage Society of Northern Colorado, CO
Swedish Heritage Society of Swedesburg, IA
Swedish Historical Society of Rockford, IL
Swedish Press Society, British Columbia, Canada
Swedish Roots in Oregon, OR
Swedish School in Marin, CA

Swedish Society Linnea, OR
Swedish Society of Calgary, Alberta, Canada
Swedish Society of San Francisco, CA
Swedish Studies Endowment Program, TX
Swedish Subcommittee of the Rhode Island Historical
  Preservation & Heritage Commission, RI
Swedish Texan, TX
Swedish Trade Council, IL
Swedish Travel & Tourism Council, NY
Swenson Swedish Immigration Research Center, IL
Swinglish Project, WI
Texas Swedish Pioneers Association, TX
The American-Scandinavian Foundation, NY
The Goldstein Museum, MN
The Lingonberries, Ontario, Canada
The Swedish Club Foundation, IL
Three Crowns American Swedish Association, ND
Town of Thorsby, AL
Tre Kronor Scandinavian Society, NE
Twin Cities Nyckelharpalag, MN
Twin Cities Swedish Folk Dancers, MN
Twin City Dalaförening, MN
TystArt, Inc., OH
United Swedish Societies, NJ
University of WA, Department of Scandinavian Studies, WA
Värmlands Förbundet, MN
Värmlands-Vännerna, NY
Vasa Museum, MN
Vasa Order of America–Grand Lodge, WA
Västergötland Society, MN
Viking Age Club, MN
Viking Male Chorus, NY

Viking Ship Restoration Committee, IL
VOA–Birka Lodge #732, MA
VOA–Bishop Hill Lodge #683, IL
VOA–Carl Larsson Lodge #739, NC
VOA–Carl Widen Lodge #743, TX
VOA–Carl XVI Gustav Lodge #716, TX
VOA–Desert Viking Lodge #682, CA
VOA–District Lodge Alberta No. 18, Alberta, Canada
VOA–Drott Lodge #168, VA
VOA–Enighet Lodge #178, CO
VOA–Eskilstuna #633, Eskilstuna, Sweden
VOA–Fokus Lodge #681, KY
VOA–Framåt Lodge #405, CA
VOA–Freja Lodge #100, NY
VOA–Frihet Lodge #401, WA
VOA–Fylgia Lodge #119, CA
VOA–Glenn T Seaborg Lodge #719, CA
VOA–Gota Lejon #251, MN
VOA–Harmoni Lodge #472, OR
VOA–Ishpeming Lodge #196, MI
VOA–Jubilee Lodge #692, FL
VOA–Jubileum Lodge #755, WI
VOA–Kronan Lodge #179, IL
VOA–Kronan Lodge #2, CT
VOA–Lindbergh Lodge #494, CA
VOA–Lindbergh Lodge #505, NY
VOA–Lindgren Lodge #754, WI
VOA–Linne Lodge #153, IN
VOA–Linnea Lodge #504, CA
VOA–Lodge Norden #233, WA
VOA–Lodge Olympic #235, NJ
VOA–Miami Lodge #554, FL

VOA–Minnesota District Lodge #7, MN
VOA–Nobel Lodge #184, OR
VOA–Nobel-Monitor Lodge #130, OH
VOA–Nordic Lodge #611, MA
VOA–Nordic Lodge #660, CA
VOA–Nordic Lodge #708, GA
VOA–Norrskenet Lodge #331, IA
VOA–North Star Lodge #145, WA
VOA–Odin Lodge #726, OR
VOA–Oscars Borg Lodge #172, PA
VOA–Phoenix Lodge #677, AZ
VOA–Red Deer Lodge #733, Alberta, Canada
VOA–Småland #618, Jönköping, Sweden
VOA–Stenland #727, NY
VOA–Svea Lodge #253, IN
VOA–Svea Lodge #348, CA
VOA–Sveaborg #449, CA
VOA–Tegnér Lodge #149, CA
VOA–Tegnér Lodge #224, MT
VOA–Thule Lodge #127, NY
VOA–Thule Lodge #467, CA
VOA–Thule Lodge Swedish Folk Dancers No. 19, NY
VOA–Travelers Vasa #758, TX
VOA–Tre Kronor Lodge #713, OR
VOA–Tryggve Lodge #88, NJ
VOA–Valhalla Lodge #715, NV
VOA–Valhalla Scandinavians Lodge #746, CA
VOA–Viking Lodge #256, CA
VOA–Viking Lodge #730, MI
VOA–Satellite Lodge #661, MI
VocalEssence, MN
Wellness of Scandinavia AB, Solna, Sweden

West Shore Scandinavian Society, MI
Western Carolinas Associates of ASF, NC

Governmental Agencies

 indicates the agency is an affiliate of the Swedish Council of America

U.S. Diplomatic and Consular Representation in Sweden

Embassy of the United States of America in Sweden

Dag Hammarskjölds Väg 31
SE-115 89
Stockholm, Sweden

Phone: 46 8 783 5300

E-mail: *StockholmWeb@state.gov*
Web: *www.usemb.se*

Swedish Diplomatic and Consular Representation in the United States

Embassy of Sweden in the United States of America

Ambassador Jan Eliasson
1501 M Street NW, Suite 900
Washington, DC 20005-1702

Phone: 202.467.2600
Fax: 202.467.2699

E-mail: *info@swedish-embassy.org*
Web: *www.swedish-embassy.org*

Swedish Consulates

Alaska

Consul Edward Bernard Rasmuson
Consulate of Sweden
P.O. Box 100-600
Anchorage, AK 99510

Phone: 907.265.2930
Fax: 907.265.2068

E-mail: *anchorage@consulateofsweden.org*

Arizona

☻ Consul Lars O. Lagerman
Consulate of Sweden
Two North Central Avenue, Suite 2200
Phoenix, AZ 85004-4406

Phone: 602.364.7450
Fax: 602.364.7070

E-mail: *llagerman@bryancave.com*

Bermuda Islands

Consul Jens Juul
Consulate of Sweden
P.O. Box HM 88
Harrington Sound
Bermuda, HS 02

Phone: 441.293.7242
Fax: 441.293.7242

California

♛ Consul General Thomas Rosander
Consulate General of Sweden
Contact: Sara Vahabi
10940 Wilshire Blvd., Suite 700
Los Angeles, CA 90024

Phone: 310.473.1495
Fax: 310.473.2229

E-mail: *sara.vahabi@consulateofsweden.org*
Web: *www.swedishoffices.com*

Consul Ulf Åke Gunnar Brynjestad
Consulate of Sweden
750 B Street, Suite 1020
San Diego, CA 92101

Phone: 619.233.1106
Fax: 619.233.9890

E-mail: *sandiego@consulateofsweden.org*

♕ Consul General Barbro S. Osher
Consulate General of Sweden
Contact: Ulla Reilly
120 Montgomery Street, Suite 2175
San Francisco, CA 94104

Phone: 415.454.1518
Fax: 415.788.6841

E-mail: *sf@consulateofsweden.org*

Colorado

Consul Donald G. Peterson
Consulate of Sweden
4242 E. Amherst Avenue
Denver, CO 80222-6702

Phone: 303.758.0999
Fax: 303.758.1091

E-mail: *denverswedconsul@worldnet.att.net*

Florida

Consul David D. North
Consulate of Sweden
P.O. Box 13094
Fort Lauderdale, FL 33316

Phone: 954.467.3507
Fax: 954.467.1731

E-mail: *fortlauderdale@consulateofsweden.org*

Georgia

♛ Consul Jill Olander

Consulate of Sweden

1800 Peachtree Street NW

Suite 615

Atlanta, GA 30309

Phone: 404.352.1285

Fax: 770.431.3316

E-mail: *atlanta@consulateofsweden.org*

Hawaii

Consul James M. Cribley

Consulate of Sweden

Mauka Tower, Suite 2600

737 Bishop Street

Honolulu, HI 96813

Phone: 808.528.4777

Fax: 808.523.1888

E-mail: *honolulu@consulateofsweden.org*

Illinois

Consul General Kerstin Lane
Consulate General of Sweden
150 N. Michigan Ave., Suite 1250
Chicago, IL 60601-7593

Phone: 312.781.6262
Fax: 312.781.1816

E-mail: *chicago@consulateofsweden.org*
Web: *www.swedenchicago.com*

Kansas

Consul Clarence L. Roeder
Consulate of Sweden
13000 Glenfield Drive
Leawood
Kansas City, KS 66209

Phone: 913.498.2443
Fax: 913.498.2443

E-mail: *kansascity@consulateofsweden.org*

Louisiana

Consul William Bradish Forsyth
Consulate of Sweden
2419 Broadway Street
New Orleans, LA 70125

Phone: 504.861.2557
Fax: 504.864.1009

E-mail: *neworleans@consulateofsweden.org*

Massachusetts

Consul Franklin Bush Mead III
Consulate of Sweden
286 Congress Street, 6th Floor
Boston, MA 02210-1038

Phone: 617.451.3456
Fax: 617.423.2057

E-mail: *boston@consulateofsweden.org*

Michigan

Consul General Lennart Johansson
Consulate General of Sweden
275 Metty Drive
Ann Arbor, MI 48103-9444

Phone: 734.913.5800
Fax: 734.913.5807

E-mail: *LenSTM@aol.com*

Minnesota

Consul General Bruce Karstadt
Consulate General of Sweden
720 Baker Building
706 Second Avenue South
Minneapolis, MN 55402

Phone: 612.332.6897
Fax: 612.332.6340

E-mail: *minneapolis@consulateofsweden.org*

Missouri

Consul Grant Richard Oscarson
Consulate of Sweden
16100 Chesterfield Pkwy West
Suite 395
Chesterfield, MO 63017

Phone: 636.537.9222
Fax: 636.537.4652

E-mail: *st.louis@consulateofsweden.org*

North Carolina

Consul Anna Blomdahl
Consulate of Sweden
4900 Falls of Neuse Road, Suite 212
Raleigh, NC 27609

Phone: 919.872.0344
Fax: 919.872.0303

E-mail: *anna.blomdahl@consulateofsweden.org*

Nebraska

Consul Thomas Joseph Lund
Consulate of Sweden
700 Service Life Building
1904 Farnam Street
Omaha, NE 68102

Phone: 402.341.3333
Fax: 402.341.3434

E-mail: *omaha@consulateofsweden.org*

New York

Consul John L. Sellstrom
Consulate of Sweden
9-11 E. 4th St., P.O. Box 50
Jamestown, NY 14701-0050

Phone: 716.484.7191
Fax: 716.484.2133

E-mail: *jamestown@consulateofsweden.org*

♛ Consul General Olle Wästberg
Consulate General of Sweden
One Dag Hammarskjöld Plaza
885 Second Ave., 45th Floor
New York, NY 10017-2201

Phone: 212.583.2550
Fax: 212.755.2732

E-mail: *generalkonsulat.new-york@foreign.ministry.se*
Web: *www.swedennewyork.com*

Publication: Quarterly newsletter, *Fresh! from Sweden*

Ohio

Consul Michael Lee Miller
Consulate of Sweden
1200 Mc Donald Investment Center
800 Superior Avenue, Suite 1200
Cleveland, OH 44114-2688

Phone: 216.622.8218
Fax: 216.241.0816

E-mail: *cleveland@consulateofsweden.org*

Oregon

Consul Mark Oliver Johnson
Consulate of Sweden
c/o Milliman USA
111 S.W. 5th Ave., Suite 2900
Portland, OR 97204-3690

Phone: 503.227.0634
Fax: 503.227.7956

E-mail: *portland@consulateofsweden.org*

Pennsylvania

Consul Agneta Hagglund Bailey
Consulate of Sweden
8 Penn Center, Suite 2001
1628 JFK Boulevard
Philadelphia, PA 19103-2125

Phone: 215.496.7200
Fax: 215.569.9535

E-mail: *philadelphia@consulateofsweden.org*

Puerto Rico

♛ Consul David Segarra Jr.
Consulate of Sweden
Menaco Building 550 #5
Luchetti Industrial, Marg Oest
Bayamon, PR 00936

Phone: 787.778.2377
Fax: 787.778.2365

E-mail: *sanjuan@consulateofsweden.org*

Texas

Consul Robert H. Alpert
Consulate of Sweden
c/o Atlas Capital
100 Crescent Court, Suite 800
Dallas, TX 75201

Phone: 214.220.9910
Fax: 214.999.6095

E-mail: *dallas@consulateofsweden.org*

Consul Jan B. Dryselius
Consulate of Sweden
2909 Hillcroft Street, Suite 515
Houston, TX 77057-5852

Phone: 713.953.1417
Fax: 713.953.7776

E-mail: *houston@consulateofsweden.org*
Web: *www.swedishcounsulate.org*

Utah

Consul Björn Åblad
Consulate of Sweden
28 South 400 East
Salt Lake City, UT 84111

Phone: 801.532.8664
Fax: 801.532.2767

E-mail: *saltlakecity@consulateofsweden.org*

Virginia

Consul Rolf Anders William
Consulate of Sweden
P.O. Box 3430
Norfolk, VA 23514

Phone: 757.446.7300
Fax: 757.625.7794

E-mail: *norfolk@consulateofsweden.org*

Virgin Islands

Consul Maria Tankenson Hodge
Consulate of Sweden
Hodge & Francois
1340 Taarneberg
Charlotte Amalie, St. Thomas, VI 00802

Phone: 340.774.6845
Fax: 340.776.8900

E-mail: *charlotteamalie@consulateofsweden.org*

Washington

Consul Jahn Ruben Oskar Hedberg
Consulate of Sweden
Swedish Cultural Center
1920 Dexter Ave. N.
Seattle, WA 98109

Phone: 206.622.5640
Fax: 206.622.1756

E-mail: *seattle@consulateofsweden.org*

Wisconsin

Consul Johan Carl Ragnar Segerdahl
Consulate of Sweden
250 E. Wisconsin Ave., Suite 800
Milwaukee, WI 53202

Phone: 414.291.7835
Fax: 414.278.1294

E-mail: *milwaukee@consulateofsweden.org*

Passport Agencies

Passport Representative

Consul Arthur Renfro Savage
Royal Norwegian Consulate
1803 Eastport Drive
Tampa, FL 33605-6709

Phone: 813.247.4550
Fax: 813.247.5220

E-mail: *consulate@arsavage.com*

Passport Agency

Birgitta Fathie
10 Cascade Creek
Las Vegas, NV 89113

Phone: 702.871.7919
Fax: 702.740.4611

Swedish Diplomatic and Consular Representation in Canada

Embassy of Sweden in Canada

Ambassador Lennart Alvin
377 Dalhousie Street
Ottawa, ON K1N 9N8

Phone: 613.241.8553
Fax: 613.241.2277

Swedish Consulates

British Columbia

Consul General Magnus Ericson
Consulate General of Sweden
#1408–1188 W. Georgia St.
Vancouver, BC V6E 4A2

Phone: 604.683.5838
Fax: 604.387.8237

E-mail: *sweden@radiant.net*

Alberta

Consul Gunilla Mugan
Consulate of Sweden
1039 Durham Avenue SW
Calgary, AB T2T 0P8

Phone: 403.541.0354
Fax: 403.244.7728

Consul Donald G. Bishop
Consulate of Sweden
c/o Bishop & McKenzie
2500, 10104–1033 Avenue
Edmonton, AB T5J 1V3

Phone: 780.426.5550
Fax: 780.426.1305

Manitoba

Consul Neil Edwin Carlson
Consulate of Sweden
1035 Mission Street
Winnipeg, MB R2J 0A4

Phone: 204.233.3373
Fax: 204.233.6938

New Brunswick

Consul Allen M. Ruben
Consulate of Sweden
281 Queen Street, Suite 200
P.O. Box 1142
Fredericton, NB E3B 5C2

Phone: 506.458.8889
Fax: 506.452.8889

Nova Scotia

👑 Consul George T. H. Cooper
Consulate of Sweden
P.O. Box 730
Halifax, NS B3J 2V1

Phone: 902.491.1150
Fax: 902.425.6350

E-mail: *ellen.stevens@mcinnescooper.com*

Ontario

Consul Lars Henriksson
Consulate of Sweden
2 Bloor Street West, Suite 504
Toronto, ON M4W 3E2

Phone: 416.963.8768
Fax: 416.923.8809

Quebec

Consul Daniel Johnson
Consulate of Sweden
McCarthy Tetrault, Le Windsor
1170 Peel Street
Montreal, QC H3B 4S8

Phone: 514.397.4444

Consul Paule Gauthier
Consulate General of Sweden
c/o Desjardins Ducharme Stein Monast
1150 Claire Fontaine, Suite 300
Quebec, QC G1R 5G4

Phone: 418.640.4437
Fax: 418.523.5391

Saskatchewan

Consulate of Sweden
Ronald E. Shirkey
2550 15th Avenue
Suite 325
Regina, SK S4P 1A5

Phone: 306.359.1000
Fax: 306.359.3300

Organizations in the United States

The organizations and institutions in this section include Swedish-American and Scandinavian-American groups, as well as other organizations—such as museums, churches, non-profit organizations, and social clubs—that promote the culture and heritage of Sweden and/or Scandinavia in the United States.

 indicates the organization is an affiliate of the Swedish Council of America

♕ Agassiz Swedish Heritage Society

Matthew Edman
44734 240th St. NW
Alvarado, MN 56710

Phone: 218.965.4854

E-mail: *matlos@wiktel.com*

President: June Mosbeck

Founded: April 1987

Description: The purpose of the society is for the members to preserve their heritage, learn about Swedish culture & history, to have a liaison with the people of Sweden and Swedish America and to have "Good Times" together doing so.

Activities: Six meetings per year. Celebrate Midsommar, Santa Lucia Festival and a pea soup supper.

Publication: Newsletter printed 3–4 times per year.

Benefits: To have educational meetings, good food and fun time together. Provide two half tuition scholarships to the Concordia College Swedish Language Camp for youth 7–11 years old.

♛ American Daughters of Sweden

Janet Nelson Geist
5120 N. Kildare Ave.
Chicago, IL 60630-2607

Phone: 773.736.6244

President: Janet Nelson Geist

Founded: 1926

Description: To keep alive and foster the heritage of Swedish culture; to stimulate an intelligent interest in civic, educational, and social affairs that advances the welfare of local and national life; to unite Swedish women in America and in Sweden in closer bonds of sympathy and good fellowship.

Activities: Monthly luncheon meetings—2nd Saturday of the month. Sponsorship of permanently endowed scholarships at the University of Chicago, Augustana College, and North Park University; sponsorship of scholarships to Concordia Language Villages in northern Minnesota.

Publication: A cookbook, *Swedish Recipes Old and New.*

♛ American Nyckelharpa Association

Rita Leydon

P.O. Box 661

Lahaska, PA 18931

Phone: 215.794.8660

E-mail: *rita@ritaleydon.com*

Web: *www.nyckelharpa.org*

President: Sheila Morris

Founded: 1995

Description: The American Nyckelharpa Association is a non-profit corporation for the preservation of and fostering of the nyckelharpa. We will conduct educational programs and activities to promote knowledge of, and interest in the nyckelharpa, and the traditional music of the nyckelharpa. We shall endeavor to provide competent instruction in playing the nyckelharpa, in the traditional music, and in the traditional dance associated with the music.

Activities: Host annual gatherings for group members, future plans to offer scholarships to nyckelharpa players.

Publication: *Nyckel Notes* (quarterly)

Benefits: Receive the quarterly magazine, as well as discounts on CD's, books and nyckelharpa strings.

♛ American Scandinavian Association at Augustana College

Loryann Eis
2037 15th St.
Moline, IL 61265

Phone: 309.762.8303
Fax: 309.762.8303

E-mail: *leis@derbytech.com*
Web: *www.augustana.edu/administration/swenson/asa*

President: John E. Norton

Founded: 1934

Description: To stimulate and promote interest in relations and culture between America and all five of the Nordic countries. To preserve the Nordic heritage in western Illinois and eastern Iowa. To advance Nordic culture in the United States, and United States culture in the Nordic countries.

Activities: Some activities include: Midsommar Fest, Kräftskiva, Lucia fest in association with Augustana College's Scandinavian Department, annual Pea Soup Supper, Bus trips to Andersonville and IKEA.

Publication: A periodic newsletter

Benefits: Opportunities to participate in ASA activities, informational newsletters, discounts on ASA trips, and occasional cooking demonstrations.

American Scandinavian Association of Illinois

Carol Beu
2821 W. Rascher Ave.
Chicago, IL 60625

Phone: 773.878.0312

♛ American Scandinavian Association of the Great Plains

A. John Pearson
P.O. Box 2765
Lindsborg, KS 67456

Phone: 785.227.2302

E-mail: *pearson@informatics.net*

President: DeVere Blomberg

Founded: October 12, 1973

Description: To promote and strengthen the cultural, educational and intellectual relations between the organization's region in the United States and the countries of Denmark, Finland, Iceland, Norway, and Sweden; to preserve the Scandinavian-American heritage; to encourage the continued recognition and observation of Scandinavian customs and folklore; to sponsor and promote contemporary activities, concerts, and events to that end.

Activities: Meetings held approximately once every two months and help with Svensk Hyllningsfest.

Publication: *American Scandinavian Association of the Great Plains*

Benefits: Subscription to *Nordic Reach* magazine and scholarships.

American Scandinavian Association of the National Capital Area, Inc.

Bernice W. Munsey
3623 N. 37th St.
Arlington, VA 22207

Phone: 703.276.8228

Web: *www.geocities.com/asanca.geo*

Founded: 1963

Description: The American Scandinavian Association (ASA) is a local non-profit cultural organization incorporated in the District of Columbia. The goals of ASA are: to promote cultural exchange between the United States and the Nordic Countries of Denmark, Finland, Iceland, Norway & Sweden; to increase understanding of the Nordic peoples and societies among Americans; and to provide a forum where people interested in Scandinavia can meet and enjoy Nordic culture and activities.

Activities: Monthly meetings (September–May), on the third Monday of the month at St. John's Church in Bethesda, MD.

Publication: Monthly newsletter

Benefits: Monthly meetings with social entertainment and cultural activities, monthly newsletter, grants & scholarships, and ASA's Scandinavian Literature Group.

American Scandinavian Council

Carol Schrader
1551 Ashland, Suite 409
Des Plaines, IL 60016

Phone: 847.635.1199

♛ American Scandinavian Heritage Foundation

Norman Owen
P.O. Box 622
Jamestown, NY 14702-0622

Phone: 716.487.1849

Founded: 1966, **Incorporated:** 1983

Description: To promote and advance the intellectual relations between the United States and Scandinavian countries; to strengthen the bonds between the residents of Scandinavian descent and all people with an interest in Scandinavia.

Publication: Monthly newsletter, *American Scandinavian Heritage Foundation*

American Scandinavian Society of New York, Inc.

Pertti J. Ripatti
317 E. 52nd St.
New York, NY 10022

Phone: 212.751.0714

American Scandinavians of Monterey Central Coast

Kjell Fongstad
P.O. Box 1081
Monterey, CA 93940

Phone: 831.372.4083

♛ American Society of Swedish Engineers

Liza Henckel
780 Third Avenue
King of Prussia, PA 19406

Phone: 610.265.4352
Fax: 610.265.4608

E-mail: *information@asse-usa.org*
Web: *www.asse-usa.org*

President: Bengt Nestell

Founded: February 11, 1888

Description: The purpose of this association shall be the maintenance of a society for the promotion of the arts and sciences connected with engineering and mechanical construction and to promote scientific progress by readings, lectures, and discussions. The society has also focused on the Swedish industry and provided important links in the exchange of information and goods between the United States and Sweden.

Activities: Dinner meetings and networking opportunities, technical and commercial presentations, annual meetings.

Publication: *ASSE Newsletter*

Benefits: Participation and involvement in all of the ASSE activities, as well as a subscription to the annual newsletter and the annual yearbook of IVA.

♛ American Swedish Historical Museum

Richard Waldron, Executive Director
1900 Pattison Avenue
Philadelphia, PA 19145-5901

Phone: 215.389.1776
Fax: 215.389.7701

E-mail: *info@americanswedish.org*
Web: *www.americanswedish.org*

Chairman: Robert E. Savage

Founded: June 2, 1926

Description: The American Swedish Historical Museum, the oldest Swedish museum in the United States, was founded in 1926 to preserve Swedish and Swedish-American cultural heritage and traditions. The museum is a place where Swedes, Swedish-Americans, and people of all nationalities, who appreciate Swedish contributions to history, art, architecture, music, science and technology, can come together.

Activities: New Sweden History Conference, Teachers' Seminar, Lucia Fest, Julbord, Ärtsoppa och Punsch, Valborgsmässoafton, Midsommarfest, annual Christmas concert by Swedish Museum Singers and an Easter workshop.

Publication: Quarterly Newsletter

Benefits: Shop discount, discount on events and activities, free admission to museum, other benefits based on membership level.

♛ American Swedish Institute (ASI)

2600 Park Avenue
Minneapolis, MN 55407

Phone: 612.871.4907
Fax: 612.871.8682

E-mail: *information@americanswedishinst.org*
Web: *www.americanswedishinst.org*

President/CEO: Bruce Karstadt; **Chair of the Board:** Dennis
Johnson

Founded: 1929

Description: Established by Swedish immigrant newspaper
publisher Swan J. Turnblad, the American Swedish Institute
is a historic house, museum and cultural center offering a
variety of exhibits, concerts, lectures, education and other

programs designed to
celebrate Swedish cul-
ture in America. The
museum is housed in
the former Turnblad
mansion, built between
1904 and 1908, which
is listed on the National
Register of Historic
Places.

The American
Swedish Institute
emphasizes the emi-
grant era in its collec-
tions of Swedish-
America and celebrates
Swedish cultural traditions while nurturing relationships
with contemporary Sweden.

Collections include: emigrant artifacts and Turnblad
memorabilia; Swedish and Swedish-American fine and deco-

rative arts (extensive holdings of woodcarvings, textiles and Swedish glass), traditional crafts, and archival materials.

Activities: Julgransplundring, Midsommar Celebration, Lilly Lorénzen Scholarship, "Bridging Ages" education outreach project, Youth Day Camp, Summer Story Time, Crayfish Party, Christmas Fairs, Membership Contest, "Christmas in Scandinavia" exhibit, "Illumination of a Saint: the Legend of Sankta Lucia" exhibit, Lutfisk dinner, Lucia Festival, Tomtenissefrukost, and a Julbord.

Publications: *ASI Posten*, published 11 times per year. Occasional newsletter: *Mellan Vänner*. 2 books and a cookbook all available for sale in the ASI Bokhandel (bookstore).

Benefits: Free Admission to the museum, discounts in the museum shop, catalog and bokhandel. A subscription to *ASI Posten*, a monthly newsletter, free or discounted admission to films, lectures, concerts, dinners and special events.

American Swedish Institute Affiliate Members:
Agassiz Swedish Heritage Society
American Swedish Institute
American Swedish Institute Women's Club
ASI Male Chorus
ASI Male Chorus Auxiliary
ASI Spelmanslag
Bemidji Affiliate of ASI
Dala Heritage Society
Dalesburg Scandinavian Association
Duluth Swedish Cultural Society
FEST!

Fox Valley Swedish Society
Friends of the ASI Archives & Library
Gustavus II Adolphus Auxiliary
Idun Guild
Isanti County Historical Society
Kichi-Saga Swedish Club
North Central Iowa Svenska Klubben
Punschklubben
Scandinavian Friends
Svea Club
Svenska Sällskapet
Svenska Sällskapets Sällskap
Svenska Vännerna, Inc.
Swedish Cultural Heritage Society of the Red River Valley
Three Crowns American Swedish Association
Twin Cities Nyckelharpalag
Twin Cities Swedish Folk Dancers
Twin City Dalaföreningen
Värmlands Förbundet
Vasa Jr. Folk Dancers
Västergötland Society
VOA–John Morton Lodge #488
VOA–Runeberg Lodge #137
VOA–Stenbock Lodge #138

American Swedish Institute Women's Club

Joyce Miller
788 Garceau Lane
Vadnais Heights, MN 55127

Phone: 651.490.3420

♛ Andrews Inc. of Princeton

Chuck Andrews
3558 Brickton Road
Princeton, MN 55371

Phone: 763.631.SAAB / 1-800-882-7220
Fax: 763.389.3875

E-mail: *chuck@andrewsofprinceton.com*
Web: *www.andrewsofprinceton.com*

Co-Owners: Chuck Andrews & Don Andrews

Founded: 1973

Description: Chuck Andrews operated the business until 1980 when Don Andrews joined the business in partnership with his father. Through the years the business has dramatically expanded to include not only a body shop, but mechanical service and a nationwide parts department catering exclusively to SAAB automobiles.

Activities: Annual open house, midsommar festival.

Publication: Quarterly Newsletter

♛ Arpi Swedish Male Chorus of Metropolitan Detroit

Bengt Brogren
Swedish Club
22398 Ruth Street
Farmington Hills, MI 48336-4249

Phone: 248.553.4593

E-mail: *bengtb@msn.com*
Web: *www.swedishclub.net*

Director: Arthur Elander

Founded: 1932

Description: Organized in the 1930s, it was the forerunner, nucleus and organizer of the Swedish Club (of Greater Detroit) and now continues as an integral part of the Swedish Club. It is dedicated to the preservation of Swedish & Scandinavian ethnicity through music & often time entertains at the Club and public events and through its A.U.S.S. association with some 24 choruses throughout the country. It uses its talents to "reach out" nationwide.

Activities: Annual Lucia, midsommar, fundraisers and multiple concerts.

Publication: Bi-monthly newsletter

👑 ASI Male Chorus

Gunnar Wikstrom
6035 Gardena Lane NE
Fridley, MN 55432

Phone: 763.571.9632

E-mail: *gunnarwik@aol.com*

President: Gunnar Wikstrom

Founded: 1936

Description: Dedicated to preserving the Swedish culture through song and the preservation of Swedish music.

Activities: Two Frukosts at the American Swedish Institute, Spring concert, Sångarfest, Lucia, Midsommar and a Christmas Fair.

Publication: Monthly newsletter, *ASI Male Chorus Update*

👑 ASI Male Chorus Auxiliary

Muriel Johnson
5908 W. 101st St.
Minneapolis, MN 55438

Phone: 952.831.4180

♛ ASI Spelmanslag

Milo Oppegard

1068 River Dr.

River Falls, WI 54022

Phone: 715.425.7136

E-mail: *moppegar@pressenter.com*

Web: *www.asispelmanslag.org*

President: Milo Oppegard

Founded: September 1985

Description: Promote Swedish folk fiddling and keeping the tradition alive by promoting the youth fiddling group "lillalag."

Activities: Regular dances and concerts at the American Swedish Institute, concerts in surrounding communities and February Winter Festival at ASI.

Publication: Monthly newsletters sent to members and friends

Benefits: Practice and public performance opportunities at ASI and other venues, and organized music performance trips to Sweden.

Astoria Scandinavian Festival

Katrina Ivanoff

P.O. Box 34

Astoria, OR 97103

Astoria Chamber of Commerce: 503.325.6311

E-mail: *katrina@astoriascanfest.com*
Web: *www.astoriascanfest.com*

Chairmen: Loran Mathews and Katrina Ivanoff

Founded: 1967

Description: To promote Scandinavian heritage.

♛ Augustana Heritage Association

Ruth Ann Deppe
1100 E. 55th St.
Chicago, IL 60615-5199

Phone: 1.800.635.1116, ext. 712
Fax: 773.256.0782

E-mail: *rdeppe@lstc.edu*
Web: *www.augustanaheritage.org*

President: Reuben Swanson

Founded: 1998

Description: The Augustana Heritage Association consists of persons, institutions and groups who value their heritage of the Augustana Evangelical Lutheran Church. The Augustana Heritage Association was organized to promote and perpetuate the heritage of the Augustana Synod.

Publications: Bi-Annual newsletter. 2 Books: *The Augustana Heritage: Recollections, Perspectives and Prospects; Songs of Two Homelands, Hymns and Liturgy of the Augustana Lutheran Tradition*

♛ Augustana Historical Society

Loryann Eis, Treasurer
2037 15th St.
Moline, IL 61265-3966

Phone: 309.762.8303

E-mail: *leis@derbytech.com*
Web: *www.augustana.edu/historical*

President: Carl Stone

Founded: 1930

Description: The Mission of the Augustana Historical Society is to preserve the three linked histories of Augustana College, of its relation to the Lutheran Church, and of Swedish American immigration and culture—through publication, presentation and the collections of written records and artifacts.

Activities: Monthly Board of Directors meetings

Publications: Periodic ASH Newsletter, plus over 45 published books.

Benefits: 10% on AHS publications, ASH premiums, AHS newsletter and participation in monthly meetings.

♛ Austin Scandinavian Club

c/o Georgia Gustafson
9010 Quail Creek Drive
Austin, TX 78758

Phone: 512.836.1802

President: Georgia Gustafson

Founded: September 23, 1949

Description: Austin Scandinavian Club is organized to promote
fellowship among those of Scandinavian descent and members of their families to stimulate interest in Scandinavian
culture, promote civic enterprises, sponsor scholarships and
help ensure peace in the world by fostering closer bonds of
unity and friendship among democratic peoples of the
world.

Benefits: Fellowship and learning about one's heritage

♛ Bemidji Affiliate of ASI

Lloyd Johnson
208 Norwood Dr. NE
Bemidji, MN 56601

Phone: 218.444.3469
Fax: 708.810.6794

E-mail: *lloydwj@webtv.net*

President: Lloyd Johnson

Founded: April 1976

Description: ASI-Bemidji was the first established affiliate of the American Swedish Institute in Minneapolis, MN. Located in north central Minnesota, ASI-Bemidji provides an opportunity for persons of the area interested in Swedish heritage to belong to an organization that preserved the Swedish heritage and to educate both young and old as to the influence this has had on today's culture.

Activities: Ten monthly meetings per year; annual meeting in April; Midsommar Fest in June; St. Lucia Fest with Smörgåsbord breakfast; sponsorship of scholarships to children attending Sjölunden Swedish language camps.

Publication: Newsletter, *Nordstjärnan*, published nine times per year.

♛ Bethel Lutheran Church

Rev. Dr. Maxine M. Washington
130 N. Keeler
Chicago, IL 60624

Phone: 773.533.3638
Fax: 773.533.3635

E-mail: *maxtony@ameritech.net*
Web: *www.bethelnewlife.org*

President: Rev. Dr. Maxine M. Washington

Description: Rowing and moving by faith

Publications: Quarterly newsletter, *Bethel Builder.* CD, "Welcome to Bethel, the Next Level"

♛ Birger Sandzén Memorial Gallery

Larry Griffis
P.O. Box 348
401 N. First St.
Lindsborg, KS 67456-0348

Phone: 785.227.2220
Fax: 785.227.4170

E-mail: *fineart@sandzen.org*
Web: *www.sandzen.org*

President: Donald Johnson

Founded: 1955

Description: The Sandzén Gallery archive is the official repository of written and taped materials and photographs for the Birger Sandzén Memorial Foundation and the Margaret S. Greenough Trust. Its collections include materials concerning Birger and Alfrida Sandzén, Margaret and Pelham Greenough, and their relatives and contemporaries, along with Sandzén Gallery non-current institutional records. The archive provides physical protection and arrangement of the materials and makes them available for research and reference

not only in the present but also in the future. It also cooper-
ates with other institutions that hold additional Sandzén
materials.

Activities: Annual board meeting, Swedish collection, holiday
gift show, bi-annual hyllningsfest.

Publication: A quarterly newsletter, *Gallery Notes*

Benefits: Members receive a membership card, *Gallery Notes*,
invitations to exhibitions, previews, member events, music
programs and parties

♛ Bishop Hill Heritage Association

Michael Wendel
P.O. Box 92
103 N. Bishop Hill Rd.
Bishop Hill, IL 61419

Phone: 309.927.3899
Fax: 309.927.3010

E-mail: *bhha@winco.net*
Web: *www.bishophill.com/bhha.htm*

President: Richard Tornquist

Founded: 1962

Description: To preserve buildings, artifacts, and documents
from the colony and interpret these for the public. The
Association owns six Bishop Hill Colony buildings, which

are restored and used as a museum, apartment, craft production, and sales center. Its archives are open by appointment to scholars and families doing genealogical research.

Activities: Historical preservation; managing the museum and archives, craft demonstrations; educational programs and workshops; costumed guided tours by appointment and a museum gift shop featuring Swedish imports, Swedish food, and handmade crafts. Special events include annual "Art for Restoration" exhibits as well as other traveling exhibits.

Publication: A quarterly newsletter, *Bishop Hill Heritage Association.*

Benefits: Newsletter, 10% off gift shop, announcement of events and participation in event and workshops.

♔ Bridge to Sweden

Marie Louise Bratt
54 Washington Ave.
Endicott, NY 13760

E-mail: *mlbratt@bridgetosweden.com*
Web: *www.bridgetosweden.com*

Founded: 1999

Description: Using Internet to help people find where emigrants came from and to help find family in Sweden. Includes translations and E-mail correspondence.

Activities: Trips to Sweden in small groups—no more than seven people. Go to specific areas and parishes, farms and churches.

Publication: E-mail newsletter

♔ Cadillac Area Scandinavian Society

Guy R. Benson
5911 Sugar Bush Ln.
Cadillac, MI 49601

Phone: 231.862.3725

President: Guy Benson

Founded: 1979

Description: The Scandinavian Society seeks to foster and preserve the cultural heritage of the Scandinavian countries; to educate the general public about these customs and practices, and to provide fellowship among those who are dedicated to the preservation of these ethnic values.

Activities: Six dinner meetings per year, a St. Lucia festival, smörgåsbord, Midsummer fest, Sister City relationships, sponsorship of a concert and a food booth at the Cadillac Council of the Arts art festival and participation in various parades throughout the year.

Publication: Bi-monthly newsletter, *The Nordic Horn*

♛ Carl Sandburg Historic Site Association

Steve Holden

331 E. Third St.

Galesburg, IL 61401

Phone: 309.342.2361

E-mail: *carl@sandburg.org*
Web: *www.sandburg.org*

Founded: 1986

Description: The Carl Sandburg Historic Site Association promotes awareness of the historical and cultural significance of Carl Sandburg and the Carl Sandburg Historic site in Galesburg. The Carl Sandburg Historic Site supports a variety of educational programs and the collection, preservation and display of materials which demonstrate the life, times and achievements of Carl Sandburg.

Activities: Many activities throughout the year to honor and remember Carl Sandburg, such as the "Penny Parade" and Sandburg Days.

Publication: Quarterly Newsletter, *Inklings & Idlings*.

Benefits: Invitations and free admission to all concerts and special events, volunteer opportunities, newsletter, 10% of all museum store purchases, special premiums for larger donations and the knowledge that every member is helping to preserve the heritage of an outstanding American poet and historian.

♛ Central Iowa Associates of the American-Scandinavian Foundation

Charles Farr
740 16th Street
Des Moines, IA 50314-1601

Phone: 515.255.1340

E-mail: *farrch@mchsi.com*

President: Charles E. Farr
Founded: 1975
Description: Educate, primarily on Scandinavia.
Activities: Monthly meetings, Santa Lucia and Traditional meals.
Publication: Newsletter

♛ City of Lindsborg

c/o Ron Rolander
101 S. Main St., Box 70
Lindsborg, KS 67456

Phone: 1.888.227.2227
Fax: 785.227.4128

E-mail: *lindsborg@lindsborgcity.org*
Web: *www.lindsborgcity.org*

Mayor: Ron Rolander

City founded: 1869, **Incorporated:** 1879

Description: The City of Lindsborg was settled in the Spring of 1869 by a group of Swedish immigrants from the Värmland province of Sweden led by Pastor Olof Olsson. They envisioned a community rich in culture, learning, religion, business and farming. These values remain strong today as evidenced by a city that is rich in the performing and visual arts; home to Smoky Valley School District and Bethany College; Baptist, Catholic, Covenant, Lutheran and Methodist Churches thrive; a place where retail industry and businesses thrive; and agriculture continues to play an important role in the community.

Activities: Festivals, concerts and special art exhibitions are highlighted in Lindsborg.

👑 Dala Heritage Society

Doris Tensen
418 N.W. Railroad Avenue
Mora, MN 55051

Phone: 320.679.3005

President: Gordon Hallstrom

Founded: 1977

Description: The Dala Heritage Society shares the purposes and objectives of the American Swedish Institute of Minneapolis, MN.

Activities: Ärtsoppa och pannkaka luncheon; King Vasa Day program the day preceding the Vasaloppet in Mora, Minnesota; Midsummer celebration and raising of the majstång; coordination and hosting of various groups from Sweden; St. Lucia pageant in December.

Publication: A quarterly newsletter

♛ Dalesburg Scandinavian Association

Ronald Johnson
30595 University Rd.
Vermillion, SD 57069

Phone: 605.253.2575

E-mail: *rjohnson@bmtc.net*
Web: *www.angelfire.com/sd/dalesburg99*

President: Ronald Johnson

Founded: 1977

Description: Promote an interest in Scandinavia and Scandinavian-America. The Association is a community organization which is sponsored by Dalesburg Lutheran Church, rural Vermillion, South Dakota. Membership is open to anyone.

Activities: Midsummer festival, Lucia Event, pea soup and pancakes luncheon and Annual meeting.

Publications: A newsletter, *Dalesburg's News.* A book: *History of the Swedes who Settled in Clay County, South Dakota and Their Biographies,* by August Peterson (1947).

Benefit: A copy of the newsletter.

👑 Delaware Swedish Colonial Society

Earl Seppala
Hendrickson House
606 Church Street
Wilmington DE 19801

Phone: 302.652.5629

Web: *http://members.aol.com/sakerthing/sr-dscs.htm*

President: Earl Seppala

Founded: January 22, 1937

Description: To commemorate, on the twenty-ninth day of March each year, the establishment of the first permanent settlement in the state of Delaware with the landing of the Swedes on that date in the year 1638 at "The Rocks" in Wilmington. To collect, preserve and publish records relating to the history of Swedish settlements in America.

Activities: Landing day, March 29 (or closest Sunday) with a wreath ceremony and luncheon; Midsommar-joint trip to American Swedish Historical Museum, Philadelphia; Fall Kallboard in October; Lucia ceremony in Old Swedes Church, Wilmington.

Benefits: Mailings, four events per year and *Nordic Life*

♛ Detroit-Swedish Council

Ingrid Berge, Executive Secretary
P.O. Box 23
Bloomfield Hills, MI 48303-0023

Phone: 248.641.2999
Fax: 248.641.2999

E-mail: *iberge@msn.com*

President: Willow Hagans

Founded: 1963

Description: Sweden boasts a proud history, a powerful culture.
And whether you are a new arrival or a second or third generation Swedish-American, you need to be in touch with
your heritage. The Detroit-Swedish Council helps you make
that connection.

The Detroit-Swedish Council Inc. is one of the oldest
organizations of its kind in America. We were chartered in
1963, along with our colleagues in Philadelphia, San
Francisco and Delaware. We are one of the founding members of the Swedish Council of America. We coordinate program planning among the four affiliates and the Swedish
Council of America as often as possible to maximize exposure.

The Detroit-Swedish Council promotes Swedish culture,
for example, music and the arts, as well as educational programs, all with the intent of expanding the public's knowledge of the significant contributions made by Swedes and
Swedish Americans. We unite individuals born in Sweden

and other individuals interested in all things Swedish. We are actively attempting to recruit a new generation of Swedish Americans in our membership.

Activities: The Detroit-Swedish Council hosts several events throughout the year, as well as promoting linkages with other Scandinavian organizations in Michigan. We have developed four events that occur during the course of the year: a winter program, focusing on Swedish Art and/or current exhibitions in the area; a spring program, featuring music; our annual meeting that includes a brief business meeting and a program; and our famous annual authentic Swedish smörgåsbord.

Since 1972 the Detroit-Swedish Council has awarded an annual endowment, the Carl and Olga Milles Scholarship, to students at the Cranbrook Academy of Art. The Council offers additional endowments to students studying in Sweden and provides financial support to the University of Michigan, Scandinavian Studies Department. Other endowments are made on an annual basis to organizations demonstrating a specific need.

We have hosted two Swedish Council of America annual conferences, one in 1990 and one more recently in May of 2003.

Publication: In 1976, The Detroit-Swedish Council published a book entitled: *They Made a Difference*, to commemorate the visit to America by the Swedish king. The book highlights the Swedish influence in Detroit and the state of Michigan.

Benefits: A quarterly newsletter and a membership brochure

♕ Duluth Sister Cities Commission

Amy Weidman
12 E. 4th St.
Duluth, MN 55805

Phone: 218.723.3703
Fax: 218.723.3634

E-mail: *aweidman@ci.duluth.mn.us*
Web: *www.duluthsistercities.org*

Mayor: Gary L. Doty

Founded: 1986

Description: The Duluth Sister Cities Commission helps develop municipal partnerships between the city of Duluth and its sister cities. These relationships create opportunities for grassroots citizen participants to experience and explore other cultures through long-term municipal partnerships. Those arrangements generate an atmosphere in which economic development, trade, tourism, education, art, history, foreign language, international relations and global understanding may be stimulated.

Activities: Meetings held at 4:30 p.m. at the Central Hillside Community Center, 12 E. 4th St. the third Tuesday of every month.

Benefits: Mailings, official invitations to various events and reduced rates for delegate members.

♔ Duluth Swedish Cultural Society

Shirley Graham
4607 Otsego St.
Duluth, MN 55804

Phone: 218.525.4274

E-mail: *sgr4615227@aol.com*

President: Shirley Graham

Founded: 1934

Description: To promote Swedish culture and heritage through programs and social activities. Support of Duluth's Sister City program with Växjö, Sweden.

Activities: Seven monthly meetings, Midsummer Fest in June and Lucia.

Benefits: Education and friendship; appreciation of Swedish culture.

♔ Duluth Växjö Soccer Exchange, Inc.

Lynn Nelson
2142 Ponderosa Circle
Duluth, MN 55811

Phone: 218.720.3203

E-mail: *lmnelson1@charter.net*

Founded: October 2003

Description: The DVSE is a non-profit organization whose mission is to foster cultural relationships between the sister cities of Duluth, MN and Växjö, Sweden

Activities: The program accomplishes its goals by alternately hosting a youth soccer tournament each August between Växjö and Duluth, called the Sister Cities Soccer Cup.

Benefits: Exposure to a culture unlike their own, opportunity to develop lasting friendships and positive learning experiences, opportunity to learn new skills in soccer which often translates to bettering life skills.

Eriksen Translations Inc.

Sanne Grandt, Account Manager
32 Court Street, 20th Floor
Brooklyn, NY 11201

Phone: 718.802.9010
Fax: 718.802.0041

E-mail: *sanne@erikseninc.com*
Web: *www.erikseninc.com*

Founded by: Vigdis Eriksen

Founded: 1986

Description: Eriksen Translations Inc. provides multilingual services to Fortune 500 companies, financial institutions, law firms, medical and pharmaceutical companies, and the high tech and manufacturing industries.

👑 Fairmount Park Art Association

Sarah Katz, Development and Public Information Officer
1516 Walnut St., Suite 2012
Philadelphia, PA 19103-5313

Phone: 215.546.7550
Fax: 215.546.2363

E-mail: *sk@fpaa.org*
Web: *www.fpaa.org*

President: Charles E. Mather III

Chartered: 1872

Description: Fairmount Park Art Association is the nation's first private nonprofit organization, dedicated to integrating public art and urban planning. The initial purpose of the Art Association was to enhance Fairmount Park with sculptures, but its concerns soon expanded beyond the park to the city as a whole. Today, the Fairmount Park Art Association's programs and services carry out our multiple missions to commission, preserve and interpret public art in Philadelphia. The Art Association seeks to enrich the lives of Philadelphians by broadening the role that public art can play in our city.

Activities: Annual meeting and numerous programs held yearly.

Publications: Two books, *Public Art in Philadelphia and New-Land-Marks*: public art, community, and the meaning of place.

 FEST!

Barbara Anderson
6211 Cedar Lake Road
St. Louis Park, MN 55416

Phone: 952.541.9916

E-mail: *F_E_S_T@yahoo.com*

President: Cecilia Utne

Founded: May 1986

Description: A public-oriented organization presenting events dealing with contemporary Scandinavian issues. FEST's goal is to promote the Scandinavian heritage and contribute to the American Swedish Institute and the community, by introducing young adults to Scandinavian culture through programming at the American Swedish Institute.

Activities: Julfest, Soppaloppet, Semlor event, Waffeldagen, Valborgsmässoafton bonfire party, Kräftskiva, Pytt i Panna dinner. Skördefest dinner, and other social events at the American Swedish Institute.

Publication: Monthly newsletter, *FEST! News*

Benefits: Discount on FEST! events and the monthly newsletter

♛ Folklife Institute of Kansas

Mark Esping
P.O. Box 101
Lindsborg, KS 67456

Phone: 785.227.3522
Fax: 816.753.7585

E-mail: *folklifeinstitute@folklifeinstitute.com*
Web: *www.folklifeinstitute.com*

Executive Director: Mark Esping

Founded: 1989

Description: To heighten public awareness of folklife and folk art; to document the material culture and oral history of Central Kansas; to collect data and publish conclusions of folklife projects; to provide a structure and facility for other researchers to use; to promote involvement of other groups in documenting folklife in Central Kansas.

Benefits: Documentation, preservation, and presentation of folklife and sponsorship of events that achieve these goals, such as a folk art tour of Sweden, woodworking seminars, storytelling contests, and exhibit development.

♛ Forgat Mig Ej Children's Club

Sheila D'Camp
339 Bryan Drive
Cary, IL 60013

Phone: 847.639.2106

Fox Valley Swedish Children's Chorus

Marguerite Karl
42 W. 550 Hawk Circle
St. Charles, IL 60175

Phone: 630.365.0032

E-mail: *timnlinnea@worldnet.att.net*
Web: *www.foxvalleyswedishchildrenschorus.com*

Director: Marguerite Karl
Founded: 1999

♛ Fox Valley Swedish Society

June Holmqvist
527 E. Wilson Ave.
Appleton, WI 54915

Phone: 920.739.0076

E-mail: *ingvarwis@aol.com*

Vice President: June Holmquist

Founded: January 7, 1988

Description: Promote, preserve and inform about Swedish culture and language. Provide opportunity for people with interest in Sweden to get together.

Activities: Meetings the second Monday of the month and a Pea soup and pancake event in November.

♔ Friends of Cordelia Committee

Emmanuel Lutheran Church
1036 WA Street
Moscow, ID 83843

♔ Friends of Scandinavia

Jim Wilson
6400 Lasalle Lane
Raleigh, NC 27612

Phone: 919.847.5599

E-mail: *jim-wilson@mindspring.com*
Web: *www.rtnet.org/~nordic*

President: Jan Fagerberg

Founded: October 1979

Description: To provide activities and programs that broaden knowledge, understanding, and appreciation of Scandinavian culture; to preserve and keep alive the traditions of Scandinavia; to foster fellowship and friendship among persons of Scandinavian heritage and those interested in that heritage.

Activities: Meetings on the third Sunday of each month (Sept.–June), St. Lucia, lutefisk dinners and a Midsommar celebration.

Publication: A monthly newsletter, *FOS News*—available online

Friends of the ASI Archives & Library

Marge Pollack
2592 Rosetown Ct.
Roseville, MN 55113

Phone: 651.484.4467

Friends of the Swedish Cabin

Dave Andersson
P.O. Box 200
Drexel Hill, 9 Creek Rd.
Delaware Country, PA 19026

Phone: 610.623.1650

Web: *www.biderman.net/log.htm*

President: Grace Conran

Founded: 1985

Description: The Swedish Cabin is probably the oldest log house in North America, the Lower Swedish Log Cabin is the only remaining cabin of several built along Darby Creek during the era of New Sweden (1638–1655). It was a Swedish method to clear the land and use the logs to build a homestead.

Activities: Monthly meetings (Sept.–June), pea soup supper, Midsummer Day picnic, cabin crafts day and a trim-the-tree party in December.

Publication: Newsletter, published 2–3 times per year, *Cabin-Net*

Benefits: Discount on suppers, newsletter, lapel pin and a 10% discount.

♛ Gammelgården Museum

Lynne Blomstrand Moratzka
20880 Olinda Tr.
Scandia, MN 55073

Phone: 651.433.5053
Fax: 651.641.3531

Web: *www.scandiamn.com*

President: Mr. James "Moose" Malmquist

Founded: 1972

Description: Preserve, present and promote Swedish immigrant heritage. 11 acres, 5 buildings (1850–1868). Open May-December.

Activities: Swedish folk painting show/sale, midsommar dag, spelmansstämma, Annie's Swedish coffee party, lutfisk dinner, Lucia Dagen, calendar of classes and special events.

Publication: Newsletter published 3 times per year, *Tidskrift*

Benefits: Newsletter, discount in Butik, event tickets and *Nordic Reach*

♛ Genealogical Society of Salem Co., N.J. Inc.

Ruth Hall Brooks
Box 231
Woodstown, NJ 08098

Phone: 856.764.0969

E-mail: *gulllaker@aol.com*

President: Ruth Hall-Brooks

Founded: 1991

Description: Purposes of the society are to further the study of genealogy through meetings, lectures, seminars, and workshops; to promote the study of genealogy through education and active public relations; to educate and assist members in the methods and practices of genealogical research; and to encourage the public in the importance of preserving family history.

Activities: Monthly meetings (September to June).

Publications: Quarterly newsletter and published original Bible records of Salem County.

♔ Geneva Chamber of Commerce

Jean Gaines, Sherri Weitl
P.O. Box 481
8 S. Third St.
Geneva, IL 60134-0481

Phone: 630.232.6060 or 1.866.4Geneva
Fax: 630.232.6083

E-mail: *chamberinfo@genevachamber.com*
Web: *www.genevachamber.com*

Chairman: Scott Lebin, **President:** Jean Gaines

Founded: 1950

Description: To be the voice of its members and the business community on matters of economic, social and cultural concerns; and to develop, maintain and monitor selective programs of action which identify issues, provide support in areas of concern and foster community pride and recognition.

Activities: Annual meeting in November, Christmas Walk, Swedish Days, Geneva Arts Fair, Festival of Vines and "after hour" meetings monthly.

Publications: A newsletter printed 9 times per year: *Soundings*, Shopping/Dining/Lodging Brochure, Business Directory

Benefits: Business after hours, committee opportunities, business directory, monthly newsletter, Geneva website listing, Geneva women in business, Ambassador Club, industrial guide, business expo, community events and many more.

♛ Genline—Swedish Church Records Online

Agneta Rosenberg
857 West Belden Avenue
Chicago, IL 60614

Phone: 773.528.1247

E-mail: *agneta.rosenberg@genline.com*
Web: *www.genline.com*

President: Peter Wallenskog

Founded: 1995

Description: Genline was founded on the business idea of publishing historical Swedish Church Records via the Internet for genealogical research. Genline's Swedish Church Records archive consists of photographic quality images scanned from microfilm of original church records from the 16th–20th centuries. Users can measure their research progress in minutes and hours instead of weeks and months required with using the traditional method of microfilm. Subscriptions are available for individuals, genealogical societies and libraries. Currently, most of Genline's customers are in Sweden, but the service was developed with the North American market in mind and for the approximately 11 million Americans who have Swedish ancestry.

Activities: We have meetings together with libraries and genealogical and historical societies and offer presentations on doing Swedish genealogy. We also offer courses in Swedish genealogical research.

Publication: Quarterly online newsletter.

♛ Goldstein Museum

Lindsay Shen
244 McNeal Hall
1985 Buford Avenue
St. Paul, MN 55108

Phone: 612.624.3292
Fax: 612.624.2750

E-mail: *lshen@che.umn.edu*
Web: *http://goldstein.che.umn.edu*

Director: Lindsay Shen
Founded: 1976

Description: The Goldstein is an internationally recognized teaching museum and research center for interpreting the vital role of art in everyday life. The museum collects and preserves documents, exhibits clothing, textiles, decorative and graphic arts, with an emphasis on objects of the late 19th and 20th centuries. It promotes the study and enjoyment of these objects within their social, cultural, aesthetic, and historic contents.

Benefits: Members receive invitations to all exhibitions each year, newsletters and invitations to special members events.

Gustavus Adolphus Lutheran Church

James Amos
155 East Twenty-Second Street
New York, NY 10010

Founded: 1865

Gustavus II Adolphus Auxiliary

Ruth Rand
6924 Langford Drive
Edina, MN 55436

Phone: 952.931.9151

♔ Historic Preservation Trust of Berks County

Susan Yoder
P.O. Box 245
Douglassville, PA 19518

Phone: 610.385.4762

Web: *www.berksmuseums.org*

President: John Hibschman

Founded: 1964

Description: The purpose of the Historic Preservation Trust of Berks County is to save historic buildings threatened by destruction, whether it comes from decay, neglect, or in some cases, progress.

Activity: Annual county fair held in September.

Publication: A newsletter, *Old Morlatton Village Messenger*, printed 4–5 times per year

♔ House of Sweden

Susan Teeter
4819 Mt. Ashmun Dr.
San Diego, CA 92111-3927

Phone: 858.277.9587

E-mail: *dancingc@san.rr.com*

President: Dr. Carl Englund

Founded: May 12, 1935

Description: The House of Sweden is a group of people dedicated to preserving and educating the public about Swedish culture. Our goals and objectives are: to promote Swedish social and educational programs; to perpetuate and preserve Swedish culture, customs, art, songs, dances and language for future generations.

Activities: The cottages are arranged in a ring that encloses a courtyard and stage where meetings and performances are held on Sundays at 2:00 pm. Meetings are held to discuss business matters, upcoming events and other important issues for the organization and are followed by potluck dinners. Annual activities include: Eggsexa, Ethnic Food Fair, Midsummer Festival, Balboa Park Winter Nights and a Christmas Luncheon.

Publication: A quarterly newsletter, *Viking Vista*

Benefits: Members receive a subscription to *Nordic Reach* magazine and a copy of the *Viking Vista*

♛ Idun Guild

Jo Ann Swanson
6500 Wood Lake Drive #1202
Minneapolis, MN 55423

Phone: 612.861.2476

President: Laura Anderson

Founded: 1974

Description: The purpose of Idun Guild is to promote Swedish culture and share the American Swedish Institute's purpose and to provide enrichment for the members of the group in terms of their relationship to their heritage; non-sectarian, non-political and non-profit.

Activities: Meetings the first Thursday of the month (Sept.–May) at 6:30 pm at the American Swedish Institute.

♛ Indiana University School of Music

Eugene O'Brien
1201 E. Third St.
Bloomington, IN 47405

Phone: 812.855.5541
Fax: 812.856.5006

E-mail: *obriene@indiana.edu*
Web: *www.music.indiana.edu*

Executive Associate Dean: Eugene O'Brien

Description: The Indiana University School of Music is widely respected as one of the worlds most comprehensive institutions for musical studies. By providing the academic programs of a great university with the atmosphere of a conservatory, the school offers a coordinated program of study and performance that few can match.

Benefits: Mailing list for upcoming events

♛ Iowa City Swedish Club

Joanne Madsen
244 Woolf Avenue
Iowa City, IA 52246

Phone: 319.351.2595

E-mail: *jsmadsen@mchsi.com*
Web: *http://soli.inav.net/~tucker/*

Founded: 1978

Description: The Iowa City Swedish Club is an informal group
which meets for traditional Swedish holiday celebrations
such as Lucia and midsommar.

Activities: Language classes and films

Publication: A newsletter, 4–5 times per year

Benefits: A subscription to *Nordic Reach* and the camaraderie
the group provides

♛ Isanti County Historical Society

Kathy McCully
P.O. Box 525
139 E. 1st Ave.
Cambridge, MN 55008

Phone: 763.689.4229
Fax: 763.552.0740

E-mail: *ichs@nsatel.net*
Web: *www.ichs.ws*

Director: Valorie Arrowsmith

Founded: 1986

Description: The mission of the Isanti County Historical Society is to discover, preserve and disseminate knowledge about the history of Isanti County and the state of Minnesota.

Jackson Scandinavian American Society

Mrs. Vivian E. Rittenhouse
3137 Halstead Blvd.
Jackson, MI 49203-2553

Phone: 517.531.3271 or 517.529.9831
Fax: 517.529.9958

President: Mrs. Vivian E. Rittenhouse

Founded: 1976

Description: To further knowledge, understanding, and traditions of Scandinavian culture; to promote good fellowship among its members and the community.

Publication: Cookbook: 150-pages of heritage recipes

♛ Jacobson House Native Art Center

John Parish
609 Chautauqua Avenue
Norman, OK 73069

Phone: 405.366.1667

E-mail: *parrish968@aol.com*
Web: *www.jacobsonhouse.com*

Executive Director: John Parish

Founded: 1986

Description: Our mission is to showcase American Indian time art and culture, to preserve the legacy of Oscar Brousse Jacobson (1882–1966), and to serve the public. Jacobson was born in Västervik, Sweden.

Activities: Yearly Scandinavian Cultural Exhibit, Scandinavian Indian Christmas Festival, and cultural events.

♛ Jenny Lind Club of Michigan

Ann Nickoloff
16047 Weatherfield
Northville, MI 48167-2316

Phone: 734.420.2203

E-mail: *amn48167@wideopenwest.com*

President: Ann Nickoloff

Founded: April 10, 1937

Description: To unite for educational purposes individuals of Swedish birth or ancestry and others interested in Swedish art and culture in a continuing study of the past and present Swedish heritage, through sponsorship of meetings, concerts, symposia and exhibits to contribute knowledge to all.

Activities: Swedish smörgåsbord; annual bazaar with Swedish items, St. Lucia dinner dance in December, annual fundraiser and Jenny Lind concert.

Publication: A monthly newsletter

♛ John Ericsson Society

Kjell Lagerstrom
250 E. 63rd St.
New York, NY 10021-7663

Phone: 212.838.2587
Fax: 212.980.9655

E-mail: *kjellegubb@aol.com*
Web: *www.biderman.net/jesny*

Founded: 1907

Description: The objectives of the society are: to perpetuate and honor the memory of Captain John Ericsson, advance the profession of engineering and work for cooperation between the members of his profession in all countries, with special recognition of those branches of engineering wherein Captain John Ericsson's principal achievements were attained; to promote and encourage historic research concerning the life works of Captain John Ericsson; to gather and disseminate information concerning the history and life of Captain John Ericsson; to gather and preserve books and manuscripts, papers and relics relating to the history, life and works of Captain John Ericsson; to mark places of historic interest with suitable monuments and markers where such places are connected to the life of Captain John Ericsson.

Activities: Each year, the Society arranges two-three dinners with lectures related to John Ericsson's life and work.

Publication: A newsletter published three or four times per year.

♛ Kalmar Nyckel Foundation

Steven D. Luthultz
1124 E. 7th St.
Wilmington, DE 19801

Phone: 302.429.7447 (SHIP)
Fax: 302.429.0350

E-mail: *kalnyc@kalnyc.org*
Web: *www.kalnyc.org* or *www.kalmarnyckel.org*

President: Richard J. Julian

Founded: 1986

Mission statement: to serve as a premier volunteer maritime organization to promote the state of Delaware, City of Wilmington and the Riverfront Development to a regional, national and international clientele as an economic development and an educational outreach platform to children, adults and families.

Vision statement: to capitalize on America's attraction to its maritime history by establishing a focal point for tourism and economic development and offering hands-on educational experiences for the benefit of the community at large. The Kalmar Nyckel Foundation will build a complex of historical, cultural and educational programs and facilities focused on the colonial beginnings of Delaware.

Publications: A seasonal newsletter

Benefits: Invitations to Foundation events/program, 10% discount on purchases at the ship's store, subscription of seasonal newsletter

♛ Key of See Storytellers

Larry Johnson
315 Georgia North
Golden Valley, MN 55427

Phone: 866.893.2637

E-mail: *elent@webtv.net*

Founded: 1982

Description: To deliver stories of humor and healing for earth and everyone. Therapeutic uses of storytelling and "teller friendly" uses of media.

Activities: World Storytelling Day on March 20th. Workshops and performances promoting people telling their own stories.

♛ Kichi-Saga Swedish Club

Marian Tuominen
967 North Shore Dr.
Forest Lake, MN 55025

Phone: 651.464.3594

Founded: 1976

Description: To promote the Swedish heritage and culture in the Chisago Lakes area; to promote Swedish entertainment groups coming to the area, by providing housing and a place to perform; to send young people to the Swedish Language Village at Sjölunden; to celebrate Swedish holidays through club activities; to provide tour guides for Swedish groups.

Activities: Waffle supper in March and konditori at Karl Oscar Days in Lindstrom. Also celebrates Valborgsmässoafton at the Gustafson farm and Midsommar at the Videen home in Shafer.

Publication: *Kichi-Saga Nyheter*

♛ Kingsburg Chamber of Commerce

Jesse R. Chambers

1475 Draper St.

Kingsburg, CA 93631-1908

Phone: 559.897.1111

Fax: 559.897.4621

Web: *www.kingsburgchamberofcommerce.org*

Executive Director: Jesse R. Chambers

Founded: 1875, **Incorporated:** 1908

Description: The chamber is dedicated to providing leadership to help promote, support and encourage local businesses and residences to work together to assure that Kingsburg is a great place to live, work and play.

Activities: The community hosts celebrations and festivals throughout the year, which feature traditional Swedish dress, food, ceremonies and entertainment.

Publication: A semi-monthly newsletter, *Swedish Village Voice*

Benefits: Ribbon-cutting ceremony, chamber mixers, gratification, referrals, economic development, legislative benefit and link to chamber website.

♚ Kittson County Historical Society

P.O. Box 100

332 East Main St.

Lake Bronson, MN 56734

Phone: 218.754.6501

E-mail: *history@wiktel.com*

Director: Cindy Adams

Founded: 1880s

♚ Lake Region Swedish Heritage Society

Betty Soper

Box 791

Devils Lake, ND 58301

Phone: 701.662.3274

Founded: 1979

Description: To preserve the Swedish heritage and culture and to learn more about modern Sweden

Activities: Lectures, musical entertainment, and an annual Midsummer smörgåsbord.

Leif Ericson Society, International

Ivar Christensen
3 Toft Woods Way
Media, PA 19063

Phone: 610.565.0619

Founded: 1926

Description: To promote Leif Ericson's discovery of North
America in 1003 and to give Leif Ericson as much credit for
showing the way as others have received for following it.

Activities: Celebration of Leif Ericson Day, annually on
October 9th, in various parts of the country; providing
speakers and appearing frequently on television and radio to
provide information about Leif Ericson.

Publication: Newsletter

Leif Ericson Viking Ship "Norseman," Inc.

Dave Segermark
4919 Township Line Road, #303
Drexel Hill, PA 19026

Phone: 602.656.8414

E-mail: info@vikingship.org
Web: www.vikingship.org

President: Marty Martinson

Founded: March, 1992

Description: The Mission of the Leif Ericson Viking Ship Norseman and its crew is threefold—

1. To educate all Americans about Leif Ericson as the first European to have discovered and settled on the North American continent.

2. To promote knowledge and a realistic image of the Viking people as merchants, navigators, shipbuilders, artists, explorers and warriors.

3. To provide sail training and practice in recreating the experience of traveling on water as the Vikings did a thousand years ago.

Activities: Attending Scandinavian events with our Viking Ship replica the Norseman. Sailing our Norseman in Tall Ship events to publicize our mission. Speaking at schools, organizations to publicize our mission.

Publication: *The Norseman News*, published twice a year

Benefits: Supporting our mission, participating in the sailing of the Viking Ship, learning about sailing in the Viking Ship, speaking at schools, living the Viking life . . . occasionally.

♛ Leif Eriksson International Festival

Pastor Jens Dale
924 21st Street
Minneapolis, MN 55404-2952

Phone: 612.874.0716
Fax: 612.874.1971

E-mail: *minkdekirken@mindekirken.org*
Web: *www.mindekirken.org/LEIF.htm*

Honorary Chair: Consul General Thor Johansen
Founded: 1987
Activity: A month-long Scandinavian festival each October.

👑 Lindsborg Chamber of Commerce

Kathy Malm
104 E. Lincoln
Lindsborg, KS 67456

Phone: 785.227.3576 or 1.888.227.2227
Fax: 785.227.3576

E-mail: *chamber@lindsborg.org*
Web: *www.lindsborg.org*

President: Tricia Hawk
Founded: 1902
Description: Experience a special blend of history and culture in Lindsborg. Old world charm springs from rich Swedish heritage. Unique shops and restaurants, museums, art galleries and working studios, cultural and ethnic events, great

places to stay and lots of friendly people await you in
Lindsborg

Activities: Many colorful events take place in Lindsborg. The
Messiah Festival of music and art is the most widely known
community event. Lindsborg's colorful Swedish-American
heritage is celebrated at the Midsummer's Day Festival, the
Lucia Fest and Svensk Hyllningsfest. Other seasonal events
include: Fourth of July celebration, Broadway RFD, chess
tournament in December, Artist exhibitions and many
others.

Publication: A newsletter, 2 times per year, *Destination
Lindsborg*

♛ Lindsborg Swedish Folk Dancers

L'Jean Swisher
104 E. Lincoln, P.O. Box 242
Lindsborg KS 67456

Phone: 785.227.3578
Fax: 785.227.2488

E-mail: *ljean_s@yahoo.com*
Web: *www.svenskhyllningsfest.org/folk_dancers.htm*

Founded: 1963

Description: The Lindsborg Swedish Folk Dancers, a group of about 40 high school-age young persons, who are recognized nationally as a unique folk dance group. Founded in 1963, the dancers learn and perform traditional Swedish folk dances.

Activities: Weekly practices and a traditional Scandinavian smörgåsbord on midsommar's day.

Publication: Swedish cookbook—currently in 7th printing

♔ Linneas of Texas

Rose Anderson
6414 Tarna Ln.
Houston, TX 77074

Phone: 713.774.6055

President: Annette Smith

Founded: 1951

Description: Linneas of Texas is a Swedish women's organization which raises money to support a presidential endowed scholarship at the University of Texas.

Publication: Two cookbooks

Little Vikings

Linda Ström

Phone: 650.968.9528

E-mail: *littlevikings-owner@siliconvikings.com*
Web: *www.siliconvikings.com/little_vikings/little_vikings.asp*

Description: Little Vikings is a group for Scandinavian moms, dads and children in the Silicon Valley area. We meet every Friday for play and outdoor time in parks on the Peninsula, primarily in Palo Alto, Mountain View, Sunnyvale or Los Altos.

Long Island Scandinavian Society

Doris Sclaich
P.O. Box 376
Freeport, NY 11520

Phone: 516.764.9272

Founded: 1979

Description: To plan interesting and informative monthly programs with an informal, friendly atmosphere where all Scandinavian Americans will feel welcome.

Activities: Organizes lectures on history, literature, music and art of all Scandinavian countries. The groups encourage the preservation of daily historical documents and participates in Scandinavian festivals and celebrations.

Publication: Newsletter

♛ Lutheran Social Services

Thomas Holt
715 Falconer St.
Jamestown, NY 14701

Phone: 716.665.8128
Fax: 716.665.8132

E-mail: *lssfound@lutheran-jamestown.org*
Web: *www.lutheran-jamestown.org*

President and CEO: Thomas Holt

Incorporated: 1968

Description: Lutheran Social Services is owned and operated by the upstate New York Synod of the ELCA. Incorporated in 1968 to operate social service agencies and programs on the territory of the Synod, it is a multi faceted program serving the needs of youth with special problems, the aged who need skilled nursing care, the well elderly whose lives can be more comfortable and fulfilling through apartment living, and the developmentally disabled adult.

Manhem Club, Inc

Timothy Granförs
658 Clarence Avenue
Throgs Neck
Bronx, NY 10465

Phone: 718.767.9679

Founded: 1924

Description: To support the preservation of Scandinavian culture and traditions.

Activities: Monthly meetings, St. Lucia Fest, Midsommer, as well as many other family oriented affairs with Scandinavian music and traditions. Maintains waterfront beach property in metro New York.

Publication: Monthly Bulletin

♛ Maple Ridge Swedish Study Circle

Valorie Arrowsmith
426 389th Avenue NW
Stanchfield, MN 55080

Phone: 320.396.2147
Fax: 736.368.9422

E-mail: *varrow2@ecenet.com*

Teacher: Wayne Johnson

Founded: 1995

Description: The Maple Ridge Swedish Study Circle is a Swedish language and literature study circle, which meets every Sunday night. Students gather to read and discuss Swedish literature. There is time for coffee and gossip and grammar, too!

Activities: Meetings held every Sunday, year-round.

♛ Midwest Institute of Scandinavian Culture/Norden Folk

Gerald R. Revelle
P.O. Box 522
Eau Claire, WI 54702-0522

Phone: 715.664.8132

E-mail: *grr@concad.com*
Web: *www.nordenfolk.org*

Founded: July 5, 1960

Description: Norden Folk, continues to serve the Scandinavian community in the Upper Midwest, fostering cultural programming events in: folk, modern and classical Scandinavian music, folk and modern Scandinavian dance, gammaldans, adult and children's theatre arts, genealogy, weaving/textiles, Scandinavian wood craft/ carving, visual arts, *dalmålning* and the culinary arts.

Activities: Folk music, folk dance and Scandinavian traditions

Publication: Quarterly newsletter

Benefits: Opportunity to delve into one's Scandinavian culture by developing and working within specific disciplines in the organization. Rural landscape setting (70+ acres) in Western Wisconsin, bordered by the Chippewa River and Elk Creek, offering the opportunity for canoeing, game fishing, snow shoeing, cross-country skiing and hiking developed trails.

Minnesota Associates of the American-Scandinavian Foundation

Elaine Grahm
2032 Kentucky Avenue South
St. Louis Park, MN 55426

Phone: 612.545.7669

♛ Mt. Jewett Swedish Festival

Pam Melling
P.O. Box 671
Mt. Jewett, PA 16740

Phone: 814.778.5499

E-mail: *pam@mtjewett.com*
Web: *www.mtjewett.com/swedishfestival.html*

Co-Chairs: Roger Roesch & Bruce Sitler

Founded: 1970

Description: The Swedish festival is an annual three-day community-wide event celebrating the member's Swedish heritage. Highlights include: the crowning of this year's Royalty, Parade, Fireworks, Swedish smörgåbord, car show, amusements, arts and crafts, lots and lots of good food.

Activities: Monthly fundraisers

♛ Neighbors Abroad of Palo Alto

Sally & Ed Kiester
1015¹/₂ Braddock Ave.
Pittsburgh, PA 15218-1237

E-mail: *kiester@stanford.edu*
Web: *www.cityofpaloalto.org/artsculture/sisters.html*

Founded: January 1963

Description: Neighbors Abroad is the city of Palo Alto's official sister city organization, which promotes citizen diplomacy and international understanding. Palo Alto's sister cities are: Palo, Leyte, Philippines; Oaxaca, Mexico; Enschede, Netherlands; Linköping, Sweden, and Albi, France.

♛ New Sweden Centre

Marianne Mackenzie
Kalmar Nyckel Museum Institute
819 E. 7th Street
Wilmington, DE 19801

Founded: 1991

Description: To bring to life the rich colonial history of Delaware, Maryland, Pennsylvania and New Jersey 1638–1776. Through our interpreter's program, school visits to our Centre and outreach to schools, research and book publishing.

Activities: Annual birthday party for George Washington, and an annual meeting.

Publications: Newsletter 3x per year and 2 books

♛ New Sweden Cultural Heritage Society of Oregon and Washington

Arvis Franks
8740 S.W. Oleson Road
Portland, OR 97223

Phone: 503.244.3697
Fax: 503.244.3697

E-mail: *arvisfranks@verison.net*
Web: *www.newsweden.org*

President: Ross Fogelquist

Founded: April 1989

Description: Main goals and objectives of New Sweden: to accentuate Swedish contributions to American life; to foster historical research on Swedish settlement in America and to publish and distribute; to encourage and sponsor presentations on topics of general interest relating to the Scandinavian community; to interest people in their Swedish heritage and to involve them in cultural activities; to encourage the study of modern Sweden including its language, history, literature and arts; to foster an interest in Swedish-American history through the preservation of materials in local archives, museums and libraries; to facilitate the study of family history through Swedish Roots in Oregon and the Scandinavian Genealogical Society; to develop interest in Swedish through exchange programs and communication between the peoples of America and Sweden; to encourage schools, colleges and universities to introduce or expand Swedish studies.

Activities: Scandinavian Ball, Glad Påsk-Easter potluck, Sing Along at Fogelbo, Spring brunch with the League of Swedish Societies, Valborgsmässoafton, annual antique and garage sale at Fogelbo, Midsommar, Kräftor, Oktoberfest, Scanfeast and Auction, Lucia luncheon, Lucia fest and ScanFair.

Publication: A quarterly newsletter—also available online

♛ New Sweden Historical Society

P.O. Box 33
New Sweden, ME 04762

Phone: 207.896.5843

Founded: 1925

Description: To preserve and promote the history of the New Sweden Colony and to keep the Swedish culture and heritage alive. The sons and daughters of the New Sweden colony maintain "*kapitoleum*," three floors of which illustrate immigrant history in northern Maine. Adjacent to the old capitol are the Lindsten Stuga, a restored immigrant cabin, and the Capitol Hill School, a one-room tin-ceiling schoolhouse. The Lars Noak blacksmith shop is now open.

♛ Nisswa-Stämman

Paul Wilson
16586 Nokay Lake Road
Brainerd, MN 56401

Phone: 218.764.2994

E-mail: *pwilson@brainerd.net*
Web: *www.brainerd.net/~pwilson/nisswastamman*

Description: Nisswa-Stämman is a gathering of fiddlers, nyck-elharpa players, hardingfele players, accordionists, guitarists, vocalists, dancers and general aficionados of Scandinavian folk music here in the "New World." Folk musicians love to have an audience for their art and a "Spelmansstämma" provides the natural canvas for this happy co-mingling of folks.

♛ Noon Day Scandinavian Club

Jack Anderson
5114 Capitol Avenue
Omaha, NE 68132

Phone: 402.551.0718

President: James Thorson

Founded: 1909

Description: The Club is a patriotic and public-spirited American organization of Omaha business and professional men and women of Scandinavian birth or descent, dedicated to public service and the promotion of acquaintance and good fellowship among its members.

Activities: Vikingfest in October, Christmas Brunch in December, Pea Soup Supper in February and an Annual Banquet in April.

Benefits: Event notices

♛ Norden Club of Jamestown

Curt B. Westrom
315 N. Main St., Suite 201
Jamestown, NY 14701

Phone: 716.664.6965

E-mail: *cwestrom@netsync.net*

Founded: 1911

Description: To perpetuate the Scandinavian heritage; to promote the intellectual well-being of its members.

Norden Club of Lincoln

Dorothy Ekblad
1330 Sycamore Drive
Lincoln, NE 68510

Phone: 402.488.6018

Founded: 1947

Description: To promote fellowship among individuals of Scandinavian descent, to interest the members in preserving the best in the cultural heritage of Scandinavia.

Activities: Four dinner meetings per year, featuring speakers or programs on a Scandinavian topic, to help promote progress of the nation, state and community. Christmas smörgåsbord in December.

♛ Norden Music International

Katherine Powers
P.O. Box 174
Placentia, CA 92871

Phone: 330.836.8737 or 714.278.5341
Fax: 714.278.5341

♛ Norden Women's Club

Lois Crandall
81 E. Terrace Avenue
Lakewood, NY 14750

Founded: 1916

Description: To promote interest in things Scandinavian and to preserve the traditions, customs, and folklore of Scandinavian people; to preserve records, documents, and historical items.

Nordic Dancers

Christine Kalke
6113 42nd Place
Hyattsville, MD 20781

Phone: 301.864.1596

Activities: Meets every Wednesday evening at Highland View Elementary School, Silver Spring, MD.

Nordic Folk Dancers of Chicago

Paul Johnson
2321 West Estes
Chicago, IL 60645

Phone: 773.262.5943

E-mail: *nordic94@aol.com*

President: Paul Muhr

Founded: 1973

Description: To promote Scandinavian culture through the instruction, practice and presentation of authentic Scandinavian folk dances and music for music education of club members and the general public.

Activities: Practice every Thursday (7:30–9:30 p.m.) at the Norwood Park House—5801 North Natoma, Chicago.

♔ Nordic Heritage Museum

Marianne Forssblad, Executive Director

3014 N.W. 67th St.

Seattle, WA 98117

Phone: 206.789.5707

Fax: 206.789.3271

E-mail: *nordic@intelistep.com*

Web: *www.nordicmuseum.com*

Board President: Stig Andersen

Founded: November 1979

Description: The Nordic Heritage Museum opened its doors in 1980 in Ballard—the heart of Seattle's Nordic community. Dedicated to collecting, preserving and presenting the Nordic heritage in the Pacific Northwest, it stands today as the largest ethnic museum in the Northwest. Annually, more than 65,000 people visit its varied exhibits and programs. The Museum is housed in a 1907 red brick schoolhouse, which in its time served to educate Nordic and other immigrant families who came to this region.

Today the 51,000 square foot building is filled with exhibits that pay tribute to the early Nordic immigrants and their contributions to life in the Pacific Northwest. In addition to presenting these exhibits, the Museum sponsors a language school, many year-round children's activities, and education programs serving the area schools.

Activities: The Museum holds two annual festivals: Tivoli during the summertime and Yulefest during the Christmas Holiday Season. The Museum also maintains an ongoing schedule of fine and performing arts events, which reflect Nordic origins or influence—serving to link past, present and future.

Activities: Mostly Nordic Concert Series, Children's Heritage Camp, Tivoli/Viking Days, Northern Lights Auktion, Yulefest, Scandinavian Cooking Classes, Gingerbread House Workshop, Christmas in Scandinavia.

Publications: A bi-monthly newsletter, *Nordic News; Voices of Ballard; Woven Coverlets of Norway*

👑 Nordic Study Circle

Ann Wick
1642 Madrona Beach Road
Olympia, WA 98502

Phone: 360.867.4074
Fax: 360.867.4074

E-mail: *skogkatt@worldnet.att.net*
Web: *http://communities.southsound.com/NordicStudyCircle*

Lecture Coordinator: Howard Wick

Founded: September 1989

Description: To facilitate understanding of, as well as to stimulate interest in, Nordic and Nordic-American sites and monuments both in the Pacific Northwest and in the United States in general.

Activities: The Nordic Study Circle sponsors a series of lectures each year on topics with a Scandinavian theme.

Norsk Høstfest Association

P.O. Box 1347
Minot, ND 58702-2111

Phone: 701.852.2368
Fax: 701.838.7873

E-mail: *hostfest@minot.com*
Web: *www.hostfest.com*

President: Chester M. Reiten

Founded: 1978

Description: Sponsorship of the annual Høstfest each October in Minot, North Dakota. This ethnic festival celebrates the heritage and culture of the five Scandinavian countries from which many upper Midwest families emigrated.

Activities: Range from traditional food and culture to contemporary trade goods and talent.

North Central Iowa Svenska Klubben

Gene Person
2644 3rd Ave N.
Fort Dodge, IA 50501

Phone: 515.576.3459

Northern California Spelmanslag

Jeanne Sawyer and Jim Little
321 McKendry Dr.
Menlo Park, CA 94025-2919

Phone: 408-929-5602

E-mail: *jsawyer@sawyerpartnership.com*
Web: *http://members.aol.com/iglittle/ncs.html*

President: Jeanne Sawyer

Description: The Northern California Spelmanslag's aim is to promote Scandinavian music, dance and culture through special workshops, regular meetings, concerts and performances.

Activities: Organize and present festivals which include extensive instruction in both folk dance and music, hold regular meetings for musicians in three locations where Scandinavian folk music is taught and shared, arrange concerts/dances, and host visiting musicians.

Publications: Quarterly newsletter and 5 cassettes

Sub-organizations:

Nordahl Grieg Leikarring

Nordic Footnotes

Scandiadans

Northland Dancers (children's group)

Lois Nelson

1321 Dakota St. SE

Albuquerque, NM 87108

Phone: 505.265.7482

E-mail: *dalahorse@highstream.net*

Instructor: Rudy Ulibarri

Founded: 1974

Description: A group of children who come together to dance and enjoy Scandinavian and other European dances.

Benefits: Annual participation in the Scandinavian Club of Albuquerque's Julfest and St. Lucia programs

♛ Norwegian American Foundation

Mr. Kim Nesselquist
World Trade Center
2200 Alaskan Way, Suite 300
Seattle, WA 98121

Phone: 206.239.0135
Fax: 206.448.2033

E-mail: *naf.info@norway.com*
Web: *www.norway.com*

Description: The mission of the Norwegian American
Foundation is to further cooperation among all Norwegian-
American organizations and to strengthen the ties between
Norway and people throughout North America who through
ancestry and interest have a special relationship with Norway

Publication: Bi-weekly e-mail newsletter

Norwegian Seamen's Church (2 locations)

1035 South Beacon Street
P.O. Box 1621
San Pedro, CA 90731

Phone: 310.832.6800
Fax: 310.832.1849

E-mail: *swseamensch@earthlink.net*

Web: *www.sjomannskirken.no/sanpedro*

Founded: 1864

2454 Hyde Street

San Francisco, CA 94109

Phone: 415.775.6566

E-mail: *sanfrancisco@sjomannskirken.no*

Web: *www.kirken.org* or *www.sjomannskirken.no/sanfrancisco*

Pastor: Halfdan Bondevik

Founded: 1951

Description: The Norwegian Seamen's Mission—Sjømanns-misjonen—was established to secure the moral and religious education of Scandinavian seafarers, but also to give them a "breathing room" where a fellow countryman was available to lend an ear and give some attention. Today, the churches and their staff together with traveling pastors around the globe represent a "resource center" for all Norwegians traveling internationally.

It is open every weekday 11am–7pm, on Sunday 10am–7pm. The church offers Norwegian and Swedish newspapers and magazines, and coffee and waffles are served. There is a service every Sunday at 11am. The second Sunday each month the service is held in Swedish, the other Sundays in Norwegian.

Publication: Church Newsletter

Nytta och Nöja

John Norton

4015 36th Ave. Ct.

Moline, IL 61265

Phone: 309.736.3131

E-mail: *Jnorton785@aol.com*

Founded: 1900

Description: To preserve the Swedish heritage and language

♛ Oakland Chamber of Commerce

Marlene Anderson

P.O. Box 164

Oakland, NE 68045

Phone: 402.685.5621

Fax: 402.685.6340

Web: *www.ci.oakland.ne.us*

City Clerk: Cynthia Peterson

Incorporated as a village on April 13, 1881.

Description: Located in Burt County in northwest Nebraska,
    Oakland is named after John Oak, who settled in this area in

1855 with 23 other pioneers. Mr. Oak then assisted 5 more Swedish families to settle in the Logan Creek Valley in 1866. The village was incorporated on April 13, 1881, with 30 businesses, two banks and one printing office in operation. Oakland now has a population of 1,279 and is still growing. Basic economic activities in the Oakland area include farming, cattle and hog production, feed processing, wholesale and retail sales, construction and medical services.

Ohio Norseman

Ms. Emilie Knud-Hansen
29010 Westwood Drive
Bay Village, OH 44140

Phone: 440.871.9252

Ölandsklubben

Thyra Johnson
4 Johnson Street
Shoreham, NY 11786

Phone: 516.744.8842

President: Oddvar Skadberg
Founded: 1928

Description: To bring together people from Öland now living
in the New York area; to meet and exchange memories; to
assist each other in distress and sickness.

Activities: Various social events.

👑 Ozark Scandinavian Society of Southern Missouri

Arthur Lindeman
3700 E. Dartmoor Ct.
Springfield, MO 65802

Phone: 417.862.1682

E-mail: *Swede2@sbcglobal.net*
Web: *www.osssm.org*

President: Walt Peterson

Founded: August 4, 1986

Description: To enrich the lives of our members with the
charm and beauty of the Scandinavian culture and to
increase interest in, and knowledge of our Scandinavian heritage, including Denmark, Iceland, Finland, Norway and
Sweden.

Activities: Monthly Meetings with a program, Midsommar Fest
in June and a Julfest in December.

Publications: Quarterly newsletter, *OSSSM News.* Cookbook, *Scandinavian Memories.*

Benefits: Friendship and fellowship

Pennsville Township Historical Society

Martha Rogers and Aleasa Hogate
86 Church Landing Road
Pennsville, NJ 08070

Phone: 856.678.4453

E-mail: *pvhistorical@njcool.net*
Web: *www.pvhistorical.njcool.net/index.html*

President: Ed Grant

Founded: October 27, 1987, **Incorporated:** June 9, 1988

Description: To preserve the history of the Township of Pennsville located at the Base of the Delaware Memorial Bridge in Southern New Jersey. Pennsville was originally settled by Swedes and Finns who, by 1671, had migrated from the original New Sweden Colony, founded in the Delaware Valley at Christina (now Wilmington, Delaware), to the Eastern Shore of the Delaware River. Swedes and Finn's Point and Swedesboro, which still retain these names.

Activities: Bi-monthly membership meetings with informative lectures, trips and tours, annual banquet, participation in Salem County Historic House Tour, Farm Museum open for tours Sun. and Wed. 1–3 pm or by appointment.

Benefits: In addition to helping preserve our heritage, members receive invitations to all Society events (Trips, tours, lectures, meetings), free admission to the Farm Museum, free use of the library research material, and a subscription to the bi-monthly *Newsletter*.

👑 Positive Sweden/North America

Barbro S. Osher
413 E. Strawberry Dr.
Mill Valley, CA 94941

Phone: 415.388.8311

E-mail: *osherswed@aol.com*

Founded: 1990

Description: Positive Sweden/North America works to enhance and establish a correct and positive image of present-day Sweden through seminars, breakfast meetings, and educational conferences. The target groups are selected Americans, Swedes in North America, and, in the future, Swedish-Americans. *Positiva Sverige* in Sweden was founded in 1985 by the Employers' Organization and the Federation of Wholesalers.

Activities: Breakfast meetings and lunch seminars, all targeted towards Americans; full day education seminars to update Swedes on Sweden.

♛ Prairie Public Television

Kim Stenehjem
207 N. 5th St.
Fargo, ND 58102

Phone: 701.241.6900 or 1.800.359.6900
Fax: 701.239.7651

E-mail: *info@prairiepublic.org*
Web: *www.prairiepublic.org*

Chairman: John Q. Paulsen

Description: In addition to producing a roster of PBS programs, Prairie Public Television has been a leader in providing locally produced, award-winning programs: documentaries on the history and culture of the people of the prairie; informative programs which examine the most important issues in health, the economy and agriculture; interview shows which provide in-depth discussions with the newsmakers in politics, culture, arts and education; music programs which feature our talented area musicians.

Punschklubben

Roger Baumann
2620 Urbandale Lane
Plymouth, MN 55447

Phone: 763.449.9835

Raoul Wallenberg Committee of the US

Rachel Oestreicher Bernheim
230 Park Avenue, 7th Floor
New York, NY 10169

Phone: 212.499.2695
Fax: 212.499.2671

E-mail: *rachel@raoulwallenberg.org*
Web: *www.raoulwallenberg.org*

Chairman: Rachel Oestreicher Bernheim

Founded: 1981

Description: To perpetuate the humanitarian ideals and the
nonviolent courage of Raoul Wallenberg through the national distribution of a unique academic program, "A Study of
Heroes," an inter disciplinary curriculum for use in elementary and high schools; to help fund the efforts to determine
Raoul Wallenberg's actual fate; to bestow The Raoul
Wallenberg Award on individuals, organizations and communities that reflect Raoul Wallenberg's humanitarian spirit,
personal courage and nonviolent action in the face of enor-
mous odds.

Activities: Two awards—The Raoul Wallenberg "A Hero for
Our Time" Award, and The Raoul Wallenberg Civic
Courage Award

Publications: *A Hero for Our Time* and *Raoul Wallenberg's
Children*

♔ Rhode Island Swedish Heritage Association

Carol E. Skog
P.O. Box 1023
E. Greenwich, RI 02818

Phone: 401.828.4483

E-mail: *SkogCE@aol.com*

President: Carol E. Skog

Founded: July 2002

Description: To promote, share our Swedish culture, traditions, heritage and research the history of the Swedish immigration to Rhode Island and to develop a permanent exhibit room in the Heritage Harbor Museum.

Activities: Lucia, concerts, Swedish dinners. We sell Swedish products at Vasa summer picnics and give out membership applications to make Swedes aware of our project.

Publication: Bi-annual newsletter

Benefits: Newsletter, invitations to special events, lectures, concepts, Sankta Lucia, reduced rates of admission to events and of Swedish items sold at events.

♛ Rosmalers Association of New Mexico

Anna Creamer
2921 Candelita Ct. NE
Albuquerque, NM 87112

Phone: 505.296.8450

President: Anna Creamer

Founded: 1981

Description: The Rosmalers Association of New Mexico is a
group of painters who sponsor workshops given by various
teachers from the United States and Scandinavia.

Activity: Annual boutique in November.

Publication: Quarterly Newsletter

Benefits: Access to the Association's private library.

♛ Ryssby Committee

Paulette Brockman
First Lutheran Church
803 3rd Avenue
Longmont, CO 80501

Phone: 303.776.2704

Saami Association of North America

Susan Gunness Myers
10010 Monticello Lane North
Maple Grove, MN 55369

E-mail: *smyers@nh.cc.mn.us*

Founded: April 10, 1994

Description: To create a strong Saami presence and an understanding of the Saami people and the Saami culture in North America

Benefits: Members will get a subscription to *North American Saami Journal*

Saami Baiki Foundation

Faith Fjeld
1714 Franklin Street #100-311
Oakland, CA 94612-2408

Phone: 510.547.8279

E-mail: *saamibaiki@sinewave.com*
Web: *www.baiki.org*

President: Faith Fjeld
Founded: 1998

Description: The Foundation is a non-profit educational and charitable organization. Aims to promote an awareness of the indigenous culture of Scandinavia through education, communication, research and the arts, and to facilitate a spiritual and physical connection between the descendants of Saami immigrants to America and their Nordic relatives.

Activities: The Foundation maintains a Saami research library and a Saami cultural information office; coordinates and promotes art exhibits, concerts, book publishing, and other Saami related projects.

Publication: *Baiki Magazine*, started in 1991

 San Antonio Scandinavians

Walt Larson, Treasurer
3719 Oak Trail
San Antonio, TX 78228

Founded: May 1978

Description: To promote fellowship and stimulate interest in the history, culture and traditions of Scandinavia.

 San Francisco Performances

Allison Roe
500 Sutter Street, Suite 710
San Francisco, CA 94102

Phone: 415.398.6449
Fax: 415.398.6439

E-mail: *info@performances.org*
Web: *www.performances.org*

First season: 1980–81

Description: In 2004, San Francisco Performances celebrated 24 years as the Bay Area's leading independent presenter of chamber music, vocal and instrumental recitals, jazz and contemporary dance. Under the artistic direction of its founder, Ruth Felt, the organization presents internationally acclaimed and emerging performing artists, introduces innovative programs, and builds new and diversified audiences for the arts through education and outreach activities that also strengthen the local performing arts community.

Scandinavian Accordion Club

Jeanne Eriksson Widman
P.O. Box 0712
Baldwin, NY 11510

Phone: 718.415.0602

E-mail: *jeannewidman@aol.com*

President: Jeanne Eriksson Widman
Founded: November 1987

Description: To share with each other and the listening public the joyful sounds of Scandinavian music, interpreted by the club's original music director, composer and arranger, the late Walter Eriksson of New York, who wanted to carry on and preserve the old time dance music.

Activities: Rehearsals two times a month. The club will also play wherever invited, and has played for numerous festivals around the country.

Publications: Three musical recordings, as well as a brochure

Scandinavian American Club of Kent

Norman & Helen Perttula
425-41 Hill Drive
Aurora, OH 44202

Phone: 303.562.4370

♔ Scandinavian American Cultural & Historical Foundation

C. Allan Carlson, Secretary
4949 Tyrone Avenue #7C
Sherman Oaks, CA 91423

Phone: 818.788.4552

Founded: 1976, **Incorporated:** February 9, 1991

Description: The goals of the foundation are to preserve and exhibit Scandinavian and Scandinavia-American artifacts, folk art, books and manuscripts, provide a center for scholarly and genealogical research and recreation of the history of Scandinavian explorers.

Activities: Exhibitions, concerts, community heritage projects, lectures, research and seminars.

♛ Scandinavian American Heritage Society

Gunhild Ljung
32 Hemlock Terrace
Wayne, NJ 07470-4342

Phone: 973.696.2054

E-mail: *gljung@micronav.com*
Web: *www.sahsnj.org*

President: Bert Stromholm

Incorporated: 1977

Description: Our main goal is to foster understanding of our Scandinavian heritage and its contribution to the American Society. To promote, through programs and education, the exchange of cultural and educational activities between the Scandinavian countries and the United States of America. To offer a scholarship to a high school graduate of Scandinavian descent.

Activities: Annual Midsummer Celebration and an Annual Christmas Party.

Publication: Newsletter, 3–4 times per year

Scandinavian American Society

Harry Severson
7575 Crown Point Ave.
Omaha, NE 68134

Phone: 402.397.2084

President: Harold Olson—Council Bluffs

Founded: 1975

Description: The society is comprised of three organizations: Orvar Odd #24, Omaha Lodge #330 (VOA), and the Noon Day Scandinavian Club. The purpose of the society is to provide aid and assistance to its aged, ill and needy members and to promote the heritage, culture and traditions handed down by its forefathers.

Activities: Midsommer festival, Scandinavian folk dances, picnics, scalborg (reenactment of Vikings). The society also acts as a center for Omaha-area Scandinavian social and cultural activities, such as language classes and the annual Smörgåsbord in November.

Publication: *Scandia*—monthly publication

Benefits: Members receive an insurance policy if they are at the proper age when joining.

Scandinavian Association of Central Florida

Nils Gustafsson
3309 Monteen Drive
Orlando, FL 32806

Phone: 407.851.7314

Founded: 1977

Description: A social club that holds a monthly party, dance or picnic.

Activities: Annual St. Lucia pageant; Swedish night, which includes Swedish food, live music, and entertainment; Danish night; Norwegian night; Annual Meetings in January; various other socials; and Midsommer celebration.

Publication: A monthly newspaper

Scandinavian Association of Greater Kansas City

Torgny Andersson
436 E. 65th Terrace
Kansas City, KS 64131

Phone: 816.361.2315
Fax: 816.517.5401

Incorporated: July 1, 1994

Description: To promote understanding of the Scandinavian cultures to the general public, schools, as well as to its members.

♛ Scandinavian Center at Nansen Field

Paal Berg
P.O. Box 1492
San Pedro, CA 90733

Phone: 562.495.5262

E-mail: *Paalberg@cox.net*

Scandinavian Club of Albuquerque

Anna Creamer
2921 Candelita Court NE
Albuquerque, NM 87112

Phone: 505.296.8450

Chairman: Sharre Landa

Founded: 1972

Description: To foster interest in Scandinavian life and culture; to spread knowledge of Scandinavian history, literature, art, traditional music, and dance by means of activities and programs; to perpetuate traditions of the Scandinavian people;

to provide fellowship among members of the Club through meetings and social activities.

Activities: Monthly meetings; concerts, exhibits, films, social events; holiday celebrations such as Julfest and Midsummer fest; sponsorship of classes in language, crafts, and folk dancing; selection, purchasing and donation of books to libraries in Albuquerque; booth at Celtic Fest; contribution to Classical Literature department at the University of New Mexico; and scholarships to attend Concordia Language Villages in Minnesota.

Publications: Newsletter, *Scandinavian Club News*. The Club has compiled a bibliography of Scandinavian subject materials for the University of New Mexico Libraries, the Albuquerque public schools, and the Albuquerque public libraries.

Benefits: Provide support for Northland Dancers, children's group.

♛ Scandinavian Club of Columbus

Dr. Rudyard Whipps
283 Crestview Road
Columbus, OH 43202

Web: *www.netwalk.com/~scandiclub/*

President: Dr. Rudyard Whips
Founded: February 16, 1937

Description: The Scandinavian Club has continued to be a friendly family organization. Its members enjoy sharing their similar backgrounds and observing the traditional old Scandinavian midsummer fest, Norwegian, Danish, Finnish, Icelandic, and Swedish evenings.

Activities: Monthly dinner meetings; Columbus International Fest, Fastelavn, & Syttende Mai.

Publication: A newsletter, *Scandinews*

Benefit: Free copy of *Scandinews*

Scandinavian Club of Hawaii

Michael Melcher
6009 Kalanianaole Hwy.
Honolulu, HI 96821

Phone: 808.395.6009

E-mail: *Service@scandinavianclubofhawaii.org*
Web: *www.scandinavianclubofhawaii.org*

President: Blake Johnson

Founded: 1935

Description: The Scandinavian Club of Hawaii seeks to bring together persons with an interest in the cultures of the five Scandinavian countries, and to promote friendship between the people of Hawaii and those of Scandinavia.

Activities: Board meeting, Jul Fest, Midsommer Fest, Lucia Fest, Syttende Mai, Sailing and Hiking

Publications: Roster to Members, everything else is published online.

♛ Scandinavian Club of Hot Spring Village

Robert W. Anderson
9 Coronado Lane
Hot Springs Village, AR 71909

Phone: 501.922.4815

E-mail: *ramajo@cox-internet.com*

President: Bob Anderson

Founded: ca. 1988

Description: The club was formed to have a place for Scandinavian people to meet and associate.

Activities: Five to six meetings per year; dinner meetings and Lucia.

Scandinavian Club, Inc.

George Larson
1351 Pine Creek Road
Fairfield, CT 06430

Phone: 203.259.1571

E-mail: *inquiries@thescandinavianclub.com*
Web: *www.thescandinavianclub.com*

President: George Larson

Founded: June 3, 1916

Description: To preserve the Scandinavian culture through meetings, discussions, social dances, folk dances, singing groups, etc.

Activities: Club members enjoy social activities such as dancing, holiday celebrations, dinners, folk dancing, folk music, and Swedish language classes.

Scandinavian Collectors Club

Don Brent, Executive Secretary
P.O. Box 13196
El Canjon, CA 92022

E-mail: *dbrent@sprynet.com*
Web: *www.scc-online.org*

President: John DuBois

Founded: 1935

Description: The Scandinavian Collector's Club has developed into the world's largest specialty stamp society catering to collectors interested in philately of several Scandinavian nations. Our purpose is to promote fellowship and communication among collectors and students of Scandinavian philately.

Activities: Several stamp expos are highlighted throughout the year, as well as study groups, the Stamp Mart and the SCC library.

Publication: A quarterly newsletter, *The Post Horn*

Benefits: Not only are membership dues and donations tax deductible, but members also receive a subscription to The Post Horn. Members are allowed to freely trade stamps at the Stamp Mart, as well as utilize the SCC library and participate in study groups.

♛ Scandinavian Cultural Center

Susan Young
Pacific Lutheran University
1010 122nd Street S.
Tacoma WA 98447

Phone: 253.535.7532 or 253.535.7349
Fax: 253.536.5132

E-mail: *youngse@plu.edu*
Web: *www.plu.edu/~scancntr*

President: Janet Ruud
Founded: May 1989

Description: The purpose of the Scandinavian Cultural Center (a volunteer organization) is to bring together individuals and ethnic organizations of the Pacific Northwest to preserve the heritage and culture of the five Nordic countries (Denmark, Finland, Iceland, Norway and Sweden), to promote understanding of the immigrant experience, to strengthen ties with contemporary Nordic countries, and to support Pacific Lutheran University's Scandinavian Studies Program and the Scandinavian Immigrant Experience Collection. Active membership in the SCC is open to anyone, regardless of ethnic background, and requires the payment of annual dues as set forth by the Scandinavian Cultural Council.

Activities: The Center offers year-round programming through cultural events, classes, and exhibits. Several events are held annually: Danish Fastelavn, Norwegian Heritage Festival and Annual Spring Banquet, Swedish Sankta Lucia Fest, Norwegian Christmas Service and Nordic Christmas Party/Julfest.

Publication: Bi-monthly newsletter, *The Scandinavian Scene*

Benefits: Members receive personal invitations to "members only" events, a year's subscription to our bi-monthly newsletter, a subscription to the PLU Scene quarterly magazine, 15% discount on all Scandinavian gifts at PLU's NW and Scandinavian Gift Shop and the opportunity to volunteer at the SCC.

👑 Scandinavian Cultural Center at California Lutheran University

Richard Londgren, Director
26 Faculty Drive
Thousand Oaks, CA 91360

Phone: 805.241.0391

E-mail: *ScanCenter@clunet.edu*

Description: The Scandinavian Cultural Center contains an expansive collection of historical and cultural documents and artifacts which are available for viewing by the public.

👑 Scandinavian Cultural Center of Santa Cruz

Barbara and Chuck Olson
P.O. Box 2411
Santa Cruz, CA 95063

Phone: 831.438.4307
Fax: 831.438.4307

E-mail: *barbara@olsonconnection.com*
Web: *www.scandinavians-santacruz.org*

Chairman: Barbara Olson

Founded: June 15, 1994

Description: The main goal is to support activities that bring
Scandinavian culture to the community and Northern
California. We have a Viking Hall corporation which owns
the property of Viking Hall and a farmhouse next door
which is a rental. There are architectural plans to combine
the house and Viking Hall to have a meeting hall, library,
small meeting rooms and a kaffe hus. Financially it will be
awhile!

Activities: The Center holds about nine Board meetings each
year, community programs, symposiums, rosemaling classes
twice a year, folk dances and the occasional rummage sale.

Publication: A newsletter, *Cultural Chronicle*, published 2 times
per year

Benefits: Support Valhalla so that the monthly cultural programs can be presented to the Monterey Bay Area. Lower
cost at programs/dinners for those with membership in a
Scandinavian organization. Scandinvian organizations use
the hall free of charge; individual members rent at a discount.

♛ Scandinavian Cultural Society of Greater Hartford

Eugene Mitchell
52 Farmstead Lane
Windsor, CT 06095

Phone: 860.688.4867

E-mail: *efmctk@aol.com*

Founded: 1980

Description: To publicize and promote the study and preservation of the heritage and culture values that derive from the five Scandinavian countries.

Scandinavian Dancers of Albuquerque

Neal Nelson
1321 Dakota St. SE
Albuquerque, NM 87108

Phone: 505.265.7482

E-mail: *dalahorse@highstream.net*

Instructor: Craig Olson

Founded: 1995

Description: A group of people who like to dance socially and want to maintain their Scandinavian heritage by dancing. Members enjoy performing a variety of special dances which come from Norway and Sweden.

Activities: Perform all over New Mexico. Members have the ability to attend various dance workshops around the country and world.

♛ Scandinavian Fest Inc.

Judith Eggers
52B White St.
Eatontown, NJ 07724

Phone: 732.542.8150

E-mail: *entertain@scanfest.org*
Web: *www.scanfest.org*

President: Palmer Hval

Founded: 1985, **Incorporated:** 1995

Description: Scandinavian Fest, Inc. is an educational not-for-profit organization incorporated in New Jersey with IRS 501(c)3 status. It is staffed entirely by volunteers who produce ScanFest each year. The festival is an ethnic heritage event to promote and celebrate the cultures, heritages, contributions, and current life of the Nordic regions through appropriate crafts and gifts, handicrafts, ethnic foods, and music, dance, lectures, demonstrations, reenactments, artisans, organizational presence, and similar presentations which demonstrate and celebrate the diversity and heritages of those cultures.

Activity: Annual Scandinavian Fest, typically on the weekend of (US) Labor Day

Scandinavian Festival of Long Island

Jeanne Eriksson Widman
P.O. Box 0712
Baldwin, NY 11510

Phone: 718.415.0602

E-mail: *jeannewidman@aol.om*

President: Jeanne Eriksson Widman

Description: To share Scandinavian culture through music, song and dance, encouraging local performers, as well as visiting performers from Scandinavia to participate; to hold fundraisers in order to enhance the festival.

Activities: Presentation each summer of the "Scandinavian-American Night" on Long Island which draws 5,000–10,000 people.

Scandinavian Folk Dancers Raleigh

Rae Gulick
11008 Mason Ridge Dr.
Raleigh, NC 27614

Phone: 919.676.8607

E-mail: *rgulick@nc.rr.com*

President: Rae Gulick

Founded: 1981

Description: The group performs folk dances from Denmark, Finland, Norway, Sweden as a means to preserve, through entertainment, a vital part of the cultural heritage of these countries; to foster an audience appreciation of Scandinavian traditional ethnic dancing, performed in ethnic costumes.

Activities: The dancers have performed thoughout the state of North Carolina, and in several other Atlantic states at various festivals and events for the past 15 years. They meet bi-weekly, excluding the summer, and have 6–8 major performances throughout the year.

Publication: We are currently working on a brochure.

♛ Scandinavian Folk Festival

Gwen Axelson
715 Falconer Street
Jamestown, NY 14701

Phone: 716.665.8137

E-mail: *gaxelsom@lutheran-jamestown.org*
Web: *www.lutheran-jamestown.org*

Event Coordinator: Julie Erickson

Founded: September 6, 2002

Description: Celebrating our heritage—sharing our music, dance, crafts, food and art.

Activities: Workshops on chip carving, hardanger embroidery, nyckelharpa and fiddle, genealogy and history lectures, costume fashion show, gammaldans (old time dances), kubb lawn games, hnefatafl tournament, Scandinavian food and gift vendors, beer and wine tent and all the Swedish meatballs and pickled herring you can eat!

Scandinavian Folkdancers of Houston

Howard Phillips
9123 Timberside Dr.
Houston, TX 77025

Phone: 713.661.5619

E-mail: *hphillips@pdq.net*
Web: *www.swedishclub.org/folkdancers.htm*

Dance Director: Howard Phillips

Founded: 1972

Description: The Scandinavian Folkdancers of Houston were organized in 1972 by native-born Swedes and Texans of Scandinavian descent, most of whom lived in Galveston County. The group's stated purpose has always been to preserve and display not only Scandinavian folk dances from Sweden, Norway, Denmark, and Finland, but also other aspects of Scandinavian culture and heritage.

Activities: Throughout the years the group has performed at many events throughout Southeast and Central Texas. In addition to dancing for Scandinavian churches, clubs and events, the group has reached a wider audience by performing at various festivals around Texas and Kansas.

Benefits: Opportunity to travel and become friends with like-minded people.

♛ Scandinavian Friends

Lyn Lawson
10001 Willow Bend Dr.
Waco, TX 76712

Phone: 254.751.7113
Fax: 254.751.7144

E-mail: *tedemlyn@hot.rr.com*
Web: *www.wacocitizen.com* or *www.vikingfest.com*

President: Lyn Lawson

First met: October 1989, **Chartered:** January 2000

Description: Preservation of the culture and history of the Scandinavian countries.

Activities: Meetings the second Tuesday of each month. Participation in Viking Fest, midsummer, St. Lucia celebration, Forsgard-Olson Heritage Society and Forsgard-Olson Days.

Publication: Newsletter, *Scandinavian Friends*

Benefits: Educational and social programs, volunteer opportunities in Nordic Club events.

Scandinavian Friends

Millie Miller
2885 Knox Ave. S., Apt. 308
Minneapolis, MN 55408

Phone: 612.827.4409

Scandinavian Heritage Foundation

Priscilla Blumel
1521 S.W. Marlow Ave., Suite C
Portland, OR 97225-5101

Phone: 503.296.0842
Fax: 503.297.5882

E-mail: *shf@mindspring.com*
Web: *www.scanheritage.org*

President: Kristine Olson

Founded: 1986

Description: The Scandinavian Heritage Foundation's goal is to preserve, communicate and celebrate Scandinavian heritage and culture.

Activities: Scanfeast, ScanFair, Cook n' Eat, Friday Night Lecture Series at Portland State University, Annual Meeting, August Crawfish Festival, Genealogical class series and Scan Sampler at Portland State University.

Publication: Quarterly Newsletter, *SHF, Scandinavian Heritage Foundation*

♔ Scandinavian Heritage Society of Kentucky

Marie Hosie
1644 Donelwal Dr.
Lexington, KY 40511

Phone: 859.231.8317

President: Bill Hedberg

Founded: 1991

Description: The main goal of the Scandinavian Heritage Society of Kentucky, Inc. is to study our Scandinavian culture, create an interest, and enjoy the fellowship at meetings and Scandianvian celebrations.

Activities: Host groups from Sweden and other Scandinavian countries; Scandinavian Literary Book Club; special celebrations: Laskaianen, Syttende Mai, Midsommar, Anniversary, Annual Meeting and a Luciafest.

Benefits: Lectures, dinners, potlucks, entertainment and fellowship.

♛ Scandinavian Library, Inc.

Heidi Hipple
206 Waltham Street
Newton, MA 02465

Phone: 617.965.0621

E-mail: *info@scandinavianlibrary.org*
Web: *www.scandinavianlibrary.org*

Founded: 1994

Description: The Scandinavian Library was founded in 1994 to be a center for Scandinavians (people from Sweden, Norway, Denmark, Finland and Iceland) in the Greater Boston area and includes a library and ongoing activities.

Activities: The Scandinavian Library has arrangements almost every month ranging from talks on topics of interest, to the Scandinavian community, to parties where we enjoy Nordic food and the company of anyone interested in the Nordic people or the Nordic cultures.

Publication: Newsletter, *The Library Update*, published 5–6 times per year

Benefits: Access to a large collection of books by Nordic authors, invitations to "member-only" events, special member prices for all events, timely notice for all activities and newsletter.

♛ Scandinavian Old Time Fiddle Society

Eugene Peters, Executive Director
4127 Kingston Road
Duluth, MN 55803-1218

Phone: 218.724.6801
Fax: 218.724.6801

E-mail: *fiddleorg@aol.com*
Web: *www.scandinavianfiddlesociety.org*

President: Jane Greathouse

Description: to promote and preserve Scandinavian old time fiddle music and its heritage; to loan stringed instruments to young people to encourage them to learn more about their Scandinavian history and fiddle music; to provide teachers with a variety of stringed instruments to borrow for thirty days.

Publication: A monthly newsletter, *Scandinavian Times*

Scandinavian Playgroup—Lil-Vikingarna

Jeanette McCown
San Francisco, CA

E-mail: *jeanettemccown@yahoo.com*

 **Scandinavian Seminar**

Jacqueline Waldman, Executive Director
24 Dickinson Street
Amherst, MA 01002

Phone: 413.253.9736
Fax: 413.253.5282

E-mail: *waldman@scandinavianseminar.org*
Web: *www.scandinavianseminar.org*

President: William J. Kaufmann

Founded: 1949

Description: The Scandinavian Seminar creates international learning opportunities that draw upon our roots in Nordic-American educational exchange. We believe that learning throughout life is crucial for personal growth and that intercultural exchange is imperative for the future of our global community.

Activities: We provide Study Abroad programs in Scandinavia for American students and short-term intercultural educational programs in over 24 countries throughout Europe for people of all ages.

Scandinavian Society of Cincinnati

Birgit Jorgensen
1287 Jeremy Court
Cincinnati, OH 45240

Phone: 513.825.9358 or 513.333.2987

Web: *www.geocities.com/scansoccinci*

President: Birgit Jorgensen

Founded: June 7, 1963

Description: The Scandinavian Society of Cincinnati is an organization to promote appreciation and understanding of Scandinavian heritage and culture amongst native-born Scandinavians, persons of Scandinavian lineage, and friends of Scandinavia.

Activities: Holding regular dinner and other meetings to celebrate the traditional Scandinavian holidays and events, smorgasbords, entertainment at our meetings and elsewhere, sponsoring a Scandinavian folk dance group, and donating funds for cultural and educational activities.

Publication: Newsletter

♔ Scandinavian Society of Wichita

Rev. Maynard Peterson
P.O. Box 48291
Wichita, KS 67201-8291

Phone: 316.264.8163

President: Ms. Doris Ylander

Founded: 1936

Description: To promote the spirit of good fellowship among those members of the community interested in Scandinavia and its culture, both past and present.

♔ Seattle Chamber Players

Paul Taub
1513 25th Ave.
Seattle, WA 98122

Phone: 206.328.5010
Fax: 206.726.5183

E-mail: *paultaub@dbug.org*
Web: *www.seattlechamberplayers.org*

♛ Silicon Vikings

Kjell Olsson
5043 Graves Avenue, Suite G
San Jose, CA 95129

Phone: 408.887.9871
Fax: 408.251.2862

E-mail: *Svteam@siliconvikings.com*
Web: *www.siliconvikings.com*

Chairman: Kjell Olsson

Founded: August 1997

Description: The Silicon Viking's main goal is to be the premier networking organization in Silicon Valley and the Bay
Area for people with an interest in Sweden, technology, business and finance.

Activities: Once a month, a breakfast, a lunch or an evening
mixer is held. The Silicon Vikings also arrange more
Swedish-related events like Valborg, crayfish parties and a
Lucia morning close to Christmas.

Publication: Electronic newsletter

Benefits: Newsletter and reduced price on events.

Skandia Folkdance Society

Nick Fett
7538 19th Ave NE
Seattle, WA 98115

Phone: 206.525.8207
Fax: 206.622.8130

E-mail: *nick.fett@kpff.com*
Web: *www.skandia-folkdance.org*

President: Nick Fett

Founded by: Gordon E. Tracie on January 9, 1949

Description: "It shall be the primary object and purpose of Skandia Folkdance Society to document and preserve the traditional dances and music of the Nordic lands (namely, Denmark, the Faeroes, Finland, Iceland, Norway and Sweden); to conduct educational programs and activities which will promulgate knowledge of and promote interest in these art forms; to provide competent instruction in traditional Nordic dances; to foster the use of authentic Nordic music, both live and recorded, in all Society activities."

Activities: Meetings twice per month, dance parties, weekly dance classes, Midsommarfest, Skandia Ball, Winterdansen, Springdans Northwest and various dance and music workshops.

Smålands Förbundet

Gladyce Bergman
11139 Johnson Avenue South
Bloomington, MN 55437

Phone: 612.881.6136

Founded: 1932

Description: To provide a place for people from the province of
Småland and their descendants to meet and socialize; to sustain Swedish customs and cultures.

Activities: Six meetings per year, featuring speakers, slides,
films, music and smörgåsbord.

Society of Åland, Inc.

Jeanne Eriksson Widman
P.O. Box 0172
Baldwin, NY 11510

Phone: 718.415.0602

E-mail: *jeannewidman@aol.com*

President: Jeanne Eriksson Widman

Founded: 1914

Description: Originally, the Society's main purpose was to provide health and funeral benefits for immigrants from Åland in America. While still providing benefits, the society now concentrates on the preservation of heritage, celebration of traditions and presentation of special events concerning the Åland Islands.

Activities: Monthly membership meetings, hosting visitors and performing artists visiting New York area, Midsommar Fest, summer picnic, St. Lucia Fest, and an annual memorial service at the Church of Sweden.

👑 Sons of Norway

Eivind Heiberg
1455 W. Lake St.
Minneapolis, MN 55408

Phone: 612.821.4606 or 1.800.945.8851
Fax: 612.827.0658

E-mail: *eheiberg@sofn.com*
Web: *www.sofn.com*

President: James K. Olson

Founded: 1895

Description: Sons of Norway was organized as a fraternal benefit society by 18 Norwegian immigrants in Minneapolis, Minnesota, on January 16, 1895. The purpose and goals of the founding fathers were to protect members of Sons of Norway and their families from the financial hardships experienced during times of sickness or death in the family. Over time, the mission of Sons of Norway was expanded to include the preservation of Norwegian heritage and culture in our society. We have grown since our beginning and now encompass more than 420 local lodges with a membership of 70,000 people living in North America and Norway.

Publication: A monthly magazine, *Viking*

Benefits: Subscription to *Viking*, invitations to events, tours, and exploration of the culture and history of Norway.

Southern Florida Associates of the American Scandinavian Foundation

Helen Meyer
8305 Sunrise Lakes Blvd.
Fort Lauderdale, FL 33422

Phone: 305.742.8062

♛ Stanton Historical Society

Don Peterson
Box 231
410 Hilltop
Stanton, IA 51573-0231

Phone: 712.829.2840 or 1.877.329.2840
Fax: 712.829.2393

E-mail: *stanton@mchsi.com*
Web: *http://home.mchsi.com/~stanton/cultural.html*

President: Don Peterson

Description: The Swedish heritage and Cultural Center depicts the settlement of immigrants, especially Swedish, in south-west Iowa. It is located in the former Stanton Community building, the oldest public building in Montgomery County still in use.

Publication: A newsletter, *Heritage*

♛ Stockholm Historical Society

John G. Hede
280 Main St.
Stockholm, ME 04783

Phone: 207.896.3177

E-mail: *jhede@mfx.net*
Web: *www.aroostook.me.us*

President: Albertine Dufour

Founded: July 1976

Description: A non-profit corporation. Owns and operates Stockholm Museum. Collect, identify, preserve and display historic objects connected with the Stockholm, Maine area from its founding to the present.

Activities: Open house in the summer, Parade on the 4th of July and a Christmas Coffee Hour.

Publication: A newsletter sent once or twice per year

Benefits: Members can show their pride in their heritage

👑 Stockholm Institute

Sue Corson
N-1106 451st Street
Maiden Rock, WI 54750

Phone: 715.448.2048

Founded: 1980

Description: To collect and maintain historical artifacts of the settling families of the Stockholm, Wisconsin area and to maintain the museum building and collection.

👑 Stromsburg Chamber of Commerce

Barb Fowler
Box 1
Stromsburg, NE 68666

Phone: 402.764.2501

E-mail: *chambermail@alltel.net*
Web: *www.stromsburgnebraska.com*

Mayor: Elaine K. Westring

Description: *Välkommen till Stromsburg* (Welcome to Stromsburg), the "Swede Capital of Nebraska," located 100 miles west of Omaha, 20 miles north of Interstate 80 on the Pan-American Highway, Highway 81. Fertile farm grounds producing corn, milo and soybeans surround this rural city of 1,232 residents. Stromsburg is the largest of four towns in Polk County, with a population of 5,639.

Svea Club

Signe Fluegel
2090 Roth Pl.
White Bear Lake, MN 55110

Phone: 651.429.1012

E-mail: *pfluegel@worldnet.att.net*

♔ Sveaborg

John Johnson
1825 Deveron Rd.
Baltimore, MD 21234

Phone: 410.661.9483

Web: *http://sveaborg_2.tripod.com*

Founded: 1950

Description: Sveaborg Society is a Swedish-American organization serving Baltimore, Maryland, and the surrounding area. Our purpose is to promote Swedish traditions and holidays.

Activities: Monthly meetings at Ascension Evangelical Lutheran Church, 7601 York Road, Towson, MD.

Publication: A newsletter, *Sveaborg*, 9 times per year

SVEADAL Cabin Owners Association

Mark Hanley
8229 Croy Road
Morgan Hill, CA 95037

Phone: 415.924.4550
Fax: 415.968.5532

President: Rich Van Horn

Founded: 1972

Description: To represent the cabin owners interests regarding the operation of Sveadal to the property owner, Swedish American Patriotic League.

Activities: Host touring groups from Sweden, assist in Midsommar production and support tax-paying groups that represent the organization before governmental bodies.

Publication: A newsletter

♛ Svensk Hyllningsfest

Bill Taylor

P.O. Box 323

Lindsborg, KS 67456

Phone: 785.227.3968

Fax: 785.227.9998

Web: *www.svenskhyllningsfest.org*

Co-Chairs: Gary Hartter and Betty Holweda Nelson

Founded: 1941

Description: A biennial tribute to the Swedish pioneers who settled in the Smoky Valley; to emphasize the Swedish influence which has dominated in the community and made possible its rich heritage; to preserve and provide educational opportunities associated with the Swedish-American heritage within the Smoky Valley.

Activities: A three-day Swedish Festival held every other year featuring Swedish folk dancing from local and visiting groups, Swedish smörgåsbord, arts and craft show, Swedish food demonstrations, local musical entertainment, special headline entertainment and a parade. The festival is held in conjunction with Bethany College's homecoming.

Publications: Festival brochure; off-year informational post card; booklet which focuses on the heritage and ethnic traditions on the Smoky Valley.

Svenska Barngruppen

Sacramento, CA

Phone: 309.405.9963

E-mail: *barngruppen@swedschoolsac.org*

Svenska Kyrkan

Lena Fleischmann, Secretary
5 East 48th Street
New York, NY 10017

Phone: 212.832.8443
Fax: 212.319.1604

E-mail: *newyork@swedishchurch.net*
Web: *skut.svenskakyrkan.se/newyork/*

President: Rev. Jan Kesker

Founded: 1973

Description: The Church of Sweden New York is a branch of
the Church of Sweden, but it functions independently. The
Church of Sweden in New York depends solely on the strong
congregational donations from its large number of members.

Activities: Church Services are on Sundays at 11:00 a.m. There
are various activities during the week for young adults,
including choir, kubb, Onsdagsgruppen.

Publication: Newspaper, *Out and at Home*. Congregational newsletter, and *Kyrkobladet*—three times a year

Benefits: Presale on Lucia Tickets, discounts on tickets for SAS-drawing, voting rights at annual meetings and discounts on other events.

Svenska Lekis

Ann-Marie Ödling
East Bay, CA

Phone: 510.864.1286

E-mail: *lekis_moderator@yahoo.com*

♛ Svenska Mammor

Michelle Cadeau
1489 E. 98th Street
Brooklyn, NY 11236

Phone: 718.251.3518

E-mail: *michelle@svenskamammor.com*
Web: *www.svenskamammor.com*

President: Michelle Cadeau

Founded: November 1, 2002

Description: Svenska Mammor is an Internet site helping Swedish mothers who live abroad. Our goal is to provide a network for Swedish moms and to help them teach their children Swedish language, culture and traditions.

Activities: Classes for Swedish children, walkathons and toy drives

Svenska Sällskapet

American Swedish Institute
2600 Park Avenue
Minneapolis, MN 55407

Phone: 612.871.4902
Fax: 612.871.8682

President: Greg Anderson

Founded: 1926

Description: To gather together like-minded men for the promotion of Swedish things.

Activities: Regular meetings from September through May. Midsummer party, winter party, annual golf tournament.

Svenska Sällskapets Sällskap

Kathryn Johnson
92 Woodland Circle
Edina, MN 55425

Phone: 612.927.5371
Fax: 612.928.0250

President: Kathryn Johnson

Founded: 1932

Description: The Sällskap is an auxiliary to Svenska Sällskapet. The group is a social organization that promotes Swedish culture.

Activities: Three events per year, annual meeting and social in May, a luncheon meeting in October, annual Christmas Smörgåsbord in December

☫ Svenska Troller

Anna Antonsen
6081 Celilo Lane
Eureka, CA 95503

Phone: 707.443.7963

E-mail: *annaarn@cs.com*

Founded: May 24, 1992

Description: To learn the Swedish language and to promote fellowship and the Swedish culture.

 Svenska Vänner

Elsie Weber
417 3rd Ave. SW
Jamestown, ND 58401

Phone: 701.252.1024
E-mail: *eweber@buffalocity.net*

Founded: 1985

Description: To bring together persons with Swedish roots who are scattered around East Central North Dakota to renew an appreciation of the Swedish heritage; to share Swedish traditions; to learn about contributions made by Swedish immigrants to this country; to learn more about past and present Sweden.

Publication: A newsletter, *Svenska Vänner*

 Svenska Vännerna, Inc.

Bill Nordgren
1030 N. Armstrong
St. James, MN 56081

Phone: 507.375.4217

President: Bill Nordgren

Founded: 1979

Description: To promote all aspects of Swedish and Swedish-American heritage and culture.

Activities: Midsummer fest in June and a Lutfisk supper in October.

♔ Svenskarnas Dag

Ted Noble
5428 3rd Ave. S.
Minneapolis, MN 55419

Phone: 612.825.8808

E-mail: *teddiane@mn.rr.com*
Web: *www.svenskarnasdag.com*

Chairman: Ted Noble

Founded: 1934

Description: Svenskarnas Dag is one of the biggest Swedish festivals in the US. Many people from the Upper Midwest and Scandinavia come together to celebrate this annual event.

Activities: Svenskarnas Dag is held on the last Sunday in June at Minnehaha Park in Minneapolis, Minnesota. The day includes many events, such as: a morning church service, the raising of the midsommar pole, various singing and dancing performances by local and visiting Scandinavian groups, and the crowning of the Midsommar Queen. Authentic Swedish foods and handcrafts are also available for purchase.

 ## Svenskarnas Dag Girls Choir

Diane Noble
5428 3rd Ave. S.
Minneapolis, MN 55419

Phone: 612.825.8808

Web: *www.svenskarnasdag.com*

Director: Diane Noble
Founded: 1967

SwedeCalKids

Karin Elneborg
San Jose, CA

Phone: 408.358.0466

E-mail: *dalkulla61@hotmail.com*
Web: *http://sckids.homestead.com/Aboutsck.html*

Description: A playgroup for kids 3–6 years old with Swedish links. Only Swedish is to be spoken during the meetings with songs, games, crafts and learning about Swedish traditions and celebrations

♔ Swedes of the Grand Valley

Norm Kronvall
530 Foy Drive
Grand Junction, CO 81503

Phone: 970.245.0673

E-mail: *kron530@bresnan.net*

Founded: 1992

Description: Celebration of Swedish heritage, culture and traditions.

Activities: Spring meeting, midsummer, picnic and Christmas celebration.

Benefit: *Nordic Reach* magazine

Swedish American Athletic Association, Inc.

Warren G. Johnson
9437 South Milliard Avenue
Evergreen Park, IL 60850

Phone: 708.425.3820

Founded: 1914

Description: To unite men of Swedish birth or descent of
   sound health and good character; to aid, promote, and
   advance Swedish gymnastics and all indoor and outdoor
   athletic sports; to work for the social, moral and intellectual
   welfare and advancement of the Association and its members.

Activities: Sponsorship of two bowling teams and two golf
   clubs, celebration of Swedish holidays, and other social activities.

👑 Swedish American Central Association of Southern California

Dr. Jacqueline Ahlen, Secretary
P.O. Box 40579
Pasadena, CA 91114-7579

Phone: 626.794.0729
Fax: 626.794.7515

Founded: 1921

Description: To encourage the preservation of Swedish culture,
   traditions and customs throughout America while seeking to
   further the welfare of Swedish-American and Scandinavian
   communities.

Activity: A midsommar celebration

Swedish American Council of Boston

Rose Setterberg
770 Boylston St. #6H
Boston, MA 02199

Phone: 617.262.2657

Founded: 1943

Description: To preserve and share the rich cultural life and traditions of Sweden; to develop an understanding of the role of Sweden in world history, past and present; to strengthen relations between the United States and Sweden; and to serve as a resource center for information. The Council aims to foster educational and cultural exchange between the two countries; and to provide opportunities for the community to participate in programs of excellence and holiday celebrations. Since its founding, the Council has been affiliated with the Consulate of Sweden in Boston.

Swedish American Cultural Union

Bo Börje Jonsson
3225 Grace Street NW
Washington, DC 20007

Phone: 202.338.9246

Description: Anyone interested in Swedish-American relations. Meets for lunch.

♛ Swedish American Heritage Society of Western Michigan

Klas Hjelm
29 Pearl Street NW, Suite 127
Grand Rapids, MI 49503

Phone: 616.458.0420

E-mail: *ahs@peoplepc.com*
Web: *www.sahswm.org*

Founders: Clarence & Doris Anderson; **President:** Klas Hjelm

Founded: 1997

Description: To preserve, foster and perpetuate traditional costumes and culture of our Swedish heritage, in particular, as well as that of other Scandinavians. To promote a spirit of kinship among the Swedish-American community in the Greater Grand Rapids and West Michigan areas.

Activities: Valborgsmässoafton, Midsommar and Lucia Festival. Other events include a great variety of meetings, receptions, lectures, book discussions, picnics, dinners, and entertainments around Swedish or Scandinavian topics. Annual Meeting and Swedish Heritage Day in the State of Michigan is observed on September 15th.

Publication: A newsletter, *SAHS/WM*

♛ Swedish American Historical Association of California

Robert Johnson
1619 Sandalwood Avenue
Fullerton, CA 92835

Founded: 1977

Description: The Swedish community of California has a rich background of historical significance that is unique. So that this heritage will not be diffused or distorted, the Association desires that these historical records and events be preserved as a source of inspiration and enrichment.

♛ Swedish American Historical Society

Sonja Nelson, Office Manager
3225 W. Foster Ave, Box 48
Chicago, IL 60625

Phone: 773.583.5722

E-mail: *info@swedishamericanhist.org*
Web: *www.swedishamericanhist.org*

President: Philip J. Anderson, **Chair:** Ronald J. Johnson
Founded: 1948

Description: A not-for-profit corporation established to record and interpret the Swedish presence in America

Activities: Fall and Spring dinner/meeting, tours of Swedish-American sites around the U.S.

Publications: Quarterly newsletter, *The Swedish American Historical Quarterly.* The Society publishes and sponsors books on the history and meaning of the Swedish presence in America. Over 25 publications are available for order through their website.

Benefits: The *Quarterly*, invitations to meetings, dinners and tours, book discounts and dividend books to sustaining members and above.

👑 Swedish American Historical Society of Wisconsin

Elaine Sundberg Jackson
1445 S. 171st St.
New Berlin, WI 53151

Phone: 262.786.5972

E-mail: *esjackson@milwpc.com*

President: Marjorie Jothen

Founded: 1975

Description: To gather and preserve the history of Swedish immigrants to Wisconsin.

Activities: Quarterly general meetings with presentations of interest. Julotta and Midsommar celebrations.

♛ Swedish American Museum of Chicago

Kerstin Lane
5211 N. Clark St.
Chicago, IL 60640

Phone: 773.728.8111
Fax: 773.728.8870

E-mail: *museum@samac.org*
Web: *www.swedishamericanmuseum.org*

Executive Director: Kerstin Lane

Founded: 1976

Description: The mission of the Swedish American Museum of Chicago is to preserve Swedish heritage; educate all generations in Swedish language, culture, and traditions; and celebrate Sweden's past, present and future.

Activities: Exhibits, genealogy, classes, craft workshops, concerts, lectures, films, tours, and children's activities

Publications: Quarterly newsletter, *Flaggan*. A book: *Andersonville: A Swedish American Landmark*, by Kerstin B. Lane with Carl Isaacson

Benefits: Free admission, discounts on classes, programs, and Museum Store purchases, invitations to openings and special

events, subscription to *Flaggan*. Patron members receive
additional benefits.

👑 Swedish American Patriotic League

Michael Bray
8220 Croy Road
Morgan Hill, CA 95037

Phone: 650.851.8177

E-mail: *sveadal@osfn.org*
Web: *www.sveadal.org*

Established: 1895

Description: The Swedish American Patriotic League, a congress of local organizations, is dedicated to promoting and
perpetuating our common Swedish heritage. The league is
grateful to all officers and delegates of the League as well as
to the officers and members of all constituent organizations
for over a century of selfless devotion and labor promoting
the activities of Swedish Americans in the San Francisco Bay
Area.

Activity: The primary ongoing activity which the league sponsors is an annual Midsummer celebration held every June in
Sveadal, Morgan Hill. All organizations that are part of the
League have access to the recreational facilities in Sveadal for
their members.

Swedish American Society of Central Florida

Robert Nordin
16945 Phil C. Peters Road
Winter Garden, FL 34787

Phone: 407.656.8178
Fax: 407.839.5020

President: Robert Nordin

Founded: 1996

Description: To promote the culture and heritage of Swedish ancestry and to keep alive the traditions of the past; to provide an educational link between Swedish-Americans and modern day life in Sweden; to serve as a resource for sharing information.

Activities: Quarterly meetings, special events during the Christmas season, Midsummer, sponsorship of educational programs, trips to Sweden and places of interest in the United States.

Publication: Newsletter—published six times a year.

Swedish American Society of Tidewater

Dr. Leland Peterson
1051 Manchester Ave.
Norfolk, VA 23508

Phone: 757.489.7061

E-mail: *ldpeterson@myexcel.com*
Web: *http://members.tripod.com/~SweAmer*

President: Barbara Carlson Storaasli

Founded: May 1977

Description: The Swedish American Society of Tidewater is a social organization founded by friends to promote the cultural heritage and traditions of Sweden

Activities: Midsommar Feast and Santa Lucia

Publication: A newsletter

Swedish Ancestry Research Association (SARA)

P.O. Box 70603
Worcester, MA 01607-0603

E-mail: *SARAMembership@netscape.net*
Web: *http://SARAssociation.org*

President: Lynn Fournier

Founded: 1994

Description: The Swedish Ancestry Research Association, Inc.'s main goal is to provide individuals the opportunity to meet and share ideas with others who have similar interests. We are devoted to helping our members attain their goals through an agenda of informative speakers, workshops and publications.

Activities: Monthly meetings September to June.

Publications: Newsletter 10 times per year and a yearly *Journal*

Benefits: Receive volunteer assistance with their research, newsletter, *SARA Journal*, attendance at most meetings free of charge and invitations to various events.

Swedish Art Institute

Joan Powell
8383 East Evans Road
Scottsdale, AZ 85260

Phone: 602.998.2000
Fax: 602.998.8022

President: Robert G. Johnson

Founded: 1991

Description: The Swedish Art Institute displays and promotes Swedish visual arts, contemporary and historical in nature. Endorsing Swedish art is Swedish Art Institute's principal intention with the secondary purpose of promoting the country of Sweden.

Publication: Quarterly newsletter and annual catalog.

👑 Swedish Church Abroad — Svenska Kyrkan I Utlandet/SKUT

Ernst Jensen
72 Sea Way
San Rafael, CA 94901

Phone: 415.460.1515
Fax: 415.460.1540

E-mail: *elcousa@aol.com*

Chairman: Ernset Jensen

Founded: February 8, 1998

Description: Every second Sunday of the month with the exception of July and August, the Swedish pastor posted at the Norwegian Seaman's Church in San Pedro, the port of Los Angeles, visits San Francisco and conducts a service in Swedish at 11:00 a.m. It is a well attended service and it is encouraging to see that the service is attracting younger people and many children are baptized during the year. In addition, the Pastor officiates at weddings and memorial services. On the last Friday of the month, the church invites Scandinavian students to a dinner and on every other Wednesday a group of young Scandinavian mothers with toddlers meet. Both are well attended and popular events.

Activity: Annual fundraiser

☗ Swedish Club Foundation

Bruce Olson
340 E. Hilldale Pl.
Lake Forest, IL 60045

Founded: October 4, 1967

Description: To preserve and promote Swedish language, customs, song, music, and art; to support charities of a Swedish nature; to accumulate and preserve historical information relating to Swedish immigrants to the Untied States.

☗ Swedish Club of Denver

Margie Hausburg
11038 W. 82nd Place
Arvada, CO 80005

Phone: 303.421.1038

Web: *www.swedishclubofdenver.org*

Founded: 1958

Description: We are a group of people who desire to perpetuate the good character traits that may be found in our heritage and upbringing, no matter from where we sprang! If it is truly and honestly worth preserving.

Activities: Lucia festival, Thanksgiving dinner, Scandinavian Ball, Smörgåsbord, Midsommar, Annual Meeting, Lutfisk dinner and a Julgransplundring.

♛ Swedish Club of Detroit

Douglas Arvidson
26734 Clairview
Dearborn Heights, MI 48127

Web: *www.swedishclub.net*

President: Art Pierre

Founded: 1953

Description: The Swedish Club of Metropolitan Detroit is a
social club that serves the Scandinavian community. Among
our many members are people with Swedish, Norwegian,
Danish and Finnish ethnic backgrounds.

♛ Swedish Club of Houston

John Stavinoha
807 Mulberry Lane
Bellaire, TX 77401-3807

Phone: 713.776.5060 or **Events line:** 713.774.2739
Fax: 713.776.5262

E-mail: *lmauritzson@houston.rr.com*
Web: *www.swedishclub.org*

President: Leif Mauritzson

Founded: 1986

Description: To preserve Swedish traditions and culture.

Activities: Smörgåsbord, Lucia, Crayfish, Pea Soup and Pancakes events, and Midsommar festival.

Publication: A newsletter, *Swedish Club News,* published in odd number months, 6 times per year

♛ Swedish Club of Los Angeles

Jane Hendricks
10933 Paramount Blvd.
Downey, CA 90241

Phone: 562.862.4880

E-mail: *janehendricks@juno.com*

Founded: 1922

Description: To foster the customs and ties of the many Swedes and Swedish descendants in the Los Angeles area; to assist in the preservation of the Swedish heritage through events; to provide scholarship funds for students and institutions who are involved in these activities.

♛ Swedish Club of San Francisco and the Bay Area

Harold Carlson
319 Lunada Court
Los Altos, CA 94022-1029

Phone: 650.941.0348

E-mail: *hcarl@well.com*
Web: *www.scandinavius.com/swedishclub*

Founded: March 4, 1913

Description: A social organization for people of Swedish descent and those interested in upholding Swedish traditions

Activities: Monthly meeting on the second Wednesday of the month

Publication: A monthly newsletter, *Bulletin*

♛ Swedish Club of Sarasota

Roger Wollstadt
P.O. Box 21722
Sarasota, FL 34276

Phone: 941.925.0454

E-mail: *roger4336@aol.com*

President: Lars Ericsson

Founded: 1988

Description: To provide integration and preservation of Swedish culture in the community, and member enjoyment.

Activities: Pea Soup picnic, Midsommar, Lucia, plus other non-themed meetings.

Publication: A newsletter, *Swedish News,* published 3 times per year.

Swedish Club Women's Organization

22398 Ruth Street
Farmington Hills, MI 48336

Phone: 810.478.2563

President: Joyce Wagner

Founded: 1984

Description: The purpose of this organization is to support and assist the Swedish Club in various activities, and to help preserve the customs and culture of Sweden.

Activities: Meetings held on the second Saturday morning each month, excluding July and August. Participation in an annual Sunday brunch, Midsommar, crafts and baked good sales, as well as the Scandinavian Bazaar.

Swedish Clubs Around North Dakota (SCAND)

Elsie Weber
417 3rd Avenue SW
Jamestown, ND 58401-4126

Phone: 701.252.1024

E-mail: *eweber@buffalocity.net*

President: Betty Soper

Founded: 1989

Activities: Yearly meetings, mid-year board meeting and participation in ScandFest.

♕ Swedish Colonial Society

Ronald Hendrickson
916 Swanson St.
Philadelphia, PA 19147-4332

Phone: 856.778.8088
Fax: 856.778.5775

E-mail: *info@ColonialSwedes.org*
Web: *www.ColonialSwedes.org*

Governor: Ronald A. Hendrickson

Founded: 1909

Description: To preserve the legacy of the New Sweden Colony in America (1638–1654).

Activities: Forefathers' luncheon in April, New Sweden History Conference in November and Julmiddag in December

Publications: Bi-annual newsletter, *Swedish Colonial News,* and five books regarding the history of the first permanent Swedish settlers.

♛ Swedish Council of St. Louis

Elton Tonsing
400 Tamarack Dr.
Ballwin, MO 63011-2517

Phone: 636.394.3802

E-mail: *jantonsing@cs.com*

Founded: 1976

Description: To promote knowledge and understanding of the Swedish heritage in American life and to strengthen the cultural ties between the United States and Sweden; to promote social, educational, and cultural activities which will enhance the Swedish-American heritage in St. Louis

Publication: A newsletter, *Gult och Blått*

♛ Swedish Country Interiors

Darlene Peterson Buchanan
13742-97th Avenue NE
P.O. Box 98083
Kirkland, WA 98034

Phone: 425.821.1402
Fax: 425.820.0272

E-mail: *swedish.art@gte.net*
Web: *www.swedishcountry.com*

♛ Swedish Cultural Center, Inc.

Robert Clay
1920 Dexter Avenue N.
Seattle, WA 98109

Phone: 206.283.1077
Fax: 206.283.2970

E-mail: *swedishcc@msn.com*
Web: *www.swedishculturalcenter.org*

Executive Director: R.W. Clay

Description: The Swedish Cultural Center has several rooms
suitable for meetings, dancing, banquets, wedding receptions, etc. The seating capacities may vary between 20 to 300
depending on the specific room and type of event.

Publication: A monthly newsletter, *Swedish Center News*

Benefits: Members receive the newsletter, dining privileges, interest groups, reciprocals with various organizations.

♛ Swedish Cultural Committee, Inc.

Thomas Lund
700 Service Life Bldg.
Omaha, NE 68102

Phone: 402.341.3333
Fax: 402.341.3434

E-mail: *flglaw@qwest.net*

Founded: November 12, 1989

Description: To focus attention on Swedish contributions to the intellectual, cultural, and commercial life in the state of Nebraska and in the United States in general, and to highlight aspects of historical and modern Sweden. The goal is not only to heighten awareness of Sweden and Swedish influence in the United States, but also to enhance trade, travel and intellectual ties between the two countries.

Publications: A compilation of historical and biographical data from Swedish families, institutions and businesses in Omaha: Swedes in Omaha.

Swedish Cultural Events Committee

Swedish-American Hall
2174 Market Street
San Francisco, CA 94114

Phone: 415.964.2945

President: Dr. Ted Olsson

Description: The SCEC is a networking organization to facilitate communication and cooperation among the Swedish-American organizations in the Bay Area.

♛ Swedish Cultural Heritage Society of the Red River Valley

Earl Johnson
2910 30th Street South
Moorhead, MN 56560

Phone: 218.233.3627

Description: The purpose of the Swedish Cultural Heritage Society of the Red River Valley is to enrich members' lives through their Swedish culture and to increase the awareness and understanding of modern Swedish people in the community.

Publication: A newsletter, *Vår Dal*

♔ Swedish Cultural Society of Cleveland

Lars Eriksson
19975 Emerald View
Fairview Park, OH 44126

Phone: 440.356.0688

E-mail: *leriksson1@cs.com*

President: Lars Eriksson

Founded: October 28, 1927

Description: To fulfill the need for people of Swedish national origin to get together on the common ground of their love of Scandinavian traditions and to celebrate activities and holidays.

Activities: Regular meetings on the third Saturday of every month (September–November and January–May). These meetings are normally held at the homes of members. Midsummer in June and Lucia in December.

♔ Swedish Cultural Society of Rockford

Robert H. Borden
1325 Cosper Ave.
Rockford, IL 61107-3012

Phone: 815.968.6700

President: Betty Rottman

Founded: December 15, 1950

Description: To create a bond between Swedes and Swedish descendants residing in the area; to kindle, sustain, and strengthen interest in and love of Swedish culture and language.

Activities: 7 meetings per year

Swedish Fiddle Group

Craig Olson
4100 Ravenwood Ct. NW
Albuquerque, NM 87107

Phone: 505.345.0689

E-mail: *clolson@scandia.gov*

Leader: Craig Olson

Founded: 1989

Description: Learning and playing of Swedish fiddle tunes taught by various Swedish fiddle players, either visiting the area or at workshops around the United States.

Activities: Performing at the Scandinavian Club of Albuquerque's Julfest and playing tunes to assist the Scandinavian Dancers of Albuquerque's dances.

Swedish Folk Dance Club of Los Angeles

Ed and Carol Goller
Skandia Hall
2031 East Villa Street
Pasadena, CA

Phone: 714.892.2579

Founded: 1916

Description: To promote Swedish folk dancing in order to preserve this aspect of Swedish culture. All the members have authentic Swedish costumes and perform dances as they have been done in Sweden for hundreds of years.

Activities: Performing dances for several organizations throughout the year for both Swedish and other organization and hosting many Swedish dance clubs when they visit the United States. They also perform for various holiday celebrations in the Los Angeles area.

Swedish Folk Dancers of New York

Manhem Club
568 Clarence Avenue
Bronx, NY 10465

Phone: 718.822.8965

E-mail: *oscarssons@aol.com*
Web: *www.skandjam.com/pages/SFDNY.htm*

Founded: 1906

Description: To maintain the rich heritage of traditional Swedish folk dances, as well as other Swedish customs. The dance leader takes great care in teaching many rare and old dances from various provinces in Sweden, as well as new ones recently created.

Activities: Numerous exhibitions are performed for many organizations, multicultural festivals and events in the North East region of the United States. Practice every Thursday at 8 p.m., at the Manhem Club.

♛ Swedish Foundation of Iowa's "Swede Bend" Settlement

Ruby Erickson Hendrickson
Swedish Immigrant Museum
P.O. Box 132
Stratford, IA 50249

E-mail: *SwedeBndIA@aol.com*

♔ Swedish Genealogical Society of Minnesota

Phyllis Pladsen
5768 Olson Memorial Highway
Golden Valley, MN 55422-5014

Web: *www.rootsweb.com/~mnsgm*

President: Phyllis Pladsen

Founded: March 1983

Description: The purpose of the society is to assist members in their Swedish-American genealogical research by: holding meetings for the instruction and encouragement of the members; providing informative talks on the facet of Swedish American genealogy; helping solve individual problems with all members contributing solutions; researching the more common troublesome areas; publishing materials to aid research in Swedish ancestry.

Activities: Meetings four times per year.

Publication: A quarterly newsletter, *Tidningen*

Benefit: Newsletter

Swedish Heritage Center

Sandra Anderson
301 N. Chard Ave.
Oakland, NE 68045

Phone: 402.685.6161 or 402.685.5057

President: Mrs. Joanne Peterson

Founded: 1989

Description: The Swedish Heritage Center's purpose is to preserve history and keep alive the traditions and memories of all the pioneers who settled in Oakland

Activities: Swedish Festival (during the odd years) the first weekend in June. Three programs per year, including midsommar and Christmas.

Swedish Heritage Days Committee

Cynthia Swanson
544 West Orleans
Paxton, IL 60957

Phone: 217.379.3723

President: Cynthia Swanson

Founded: 1990

Description: The Committee holds annual Swedish heritage days during a June weekend, with dancers, historic tours and Swedish foods as well as other civic events.

Activities: Sponsors Swedish groups, and conducts meetings once a month.

♔ Swedish Heritage Society of North Dakota

Lois Matson
1801 156th Street NW
Burlington, ND 58722

Phone: 701.725.4484
Fax: 701.839.3889

E-mail: *dmatson@srt.com*

President: Loren Anderson

Founded: August 12, 1993

Description: The main objective of the Swedish Heritage Society NWND is to meet other Swedes, research genealogy, education about Swedish background, have fun, and support the Scandinavian Heritage Association.

Activities: Spring and Fall meetings, Swedish Flag Day (June 6th), Midsommar and Sankta Lucia

Publication: Newsletter

Benefits: *Nordic Reach* magazine, newsletter, and fellowship at meetings.

♛ Swedish Heritage Society of Northern Colorado

Chuck Carlson
340 East C Street
Greeley, CO 80631

Phone: 970.353.8095

Founded: 1977

Description: To promote appreciation of Swedish heritage and fellowship throughout a large region of northern Colorado

♛ Swedish Heritage Society of Swedesburg

Jane Wickham
107 James Ave.
Swedesburg, IA 52652-0074

Phone: 319-254-2317

E-mail: *swedish@lisco.com*

President: Jane Wickham

Founded: June 4, 1986

Description: The mission of the Swedish Heritage Society is to create a community which preserves its Swedish-American heritage and interprets the significance of that heritage for the present and future.

Activities: Lucia Fest, Midsummer Fest, Swedish pancake breakfasts on the first Saturdays, May-August. We also serve meals to groups over 25 who wish to have ethnic foods.

Publication: A quarterly newsletter

Benefits: The newsletter, a gift shop within the Museum and monthly meetings at the Museum.

Swedish Heritage Society of Utah

Vivianne DeYoung
2053 Camino Way
Salt Lake City, UT 84121

Phone: 801.944.4991

E-mail: *swedishheritage2@aol.com*

President: Vivianne DeYoung

Founded: 1985

Description: Our main goal is to preserve and enrich Swedish culture, language, and traditions in Utah.

Activities: Spring Soup at Easter, Valborg celebration to welcome spring, Midsummer, Crayfish Party, fall potluck dinner and Lucia.

Publication: Bimonthly newsletter

Benefits: Members receive a discount on the activities and the newsletter.

♛ Swedish Historical Society of Rockford

Leah Nelson
404 S. 3rd St.
Rockford, IL 61104

Phone: 815.963.5559
Fax: 815.963.5559

E-mail: *leah@swedishhistorical.org*
Web: *www.swedishhistorical.org*

President: Gary Anderson

Founded: 1939

Description: To collect and preserve Swedish-American history
and culture of the Rockford area.

Activities: Midsommar Fest, Youth Camp and Lucia Fest.

Publications: A monthly newsletter, *Nyheter*. An annual magazine, *Swedish Heritage*

Benefits: Admission to Museum, 10% discount in the Gift
Shop, newsletter, announcements of events and research services.

Swedish Home for the Aged, Inc.

20 Bristol Avenue
Staten Island, NY 10301-4199

Phone: 718.442.1096
Fax: 718.442.5376

E-mail: *swedhome@swedishhome.org*
Web: *www.swedishhome.org*

President: Sven Mossberg

Founded: 1909

Description: The Swedish Home for the Aged is a certified adult-care facility serving the long term residential care needs of the elderly in New York City metropolitan area.

Activities: A full calendar of activities is planned every month, including: arts & crafts, bingo, restaurant outings, exercise, movies, religious services, parties and shopping.

Swedish Medical Center–Ballard

5300 Tallman Avenue NW
Seattle, WA 98107-3985

Phone: 1.800.SWEDISH or 206.782.2700

Web: *www.swedish.org*

President: Richard Peterson

Founded: 1954

Description: The Ballard campus of Swedish Medical Center was founded in the Ballard neighborhood in 1928 as the area's first community hospital. Located five miles from the downtown area, Ballard Community Hospital steadily grew and expanded over the years, and in the 1950s, Ballard citizens raised enough money to build a new 100-bed facility. This belief in growth, progress and community support has continued since the hospital merged with Swedish Medical Center in the early 1990s.

Swedish Medical Center–First Hill

747 Broadway
Seattle, WA 98122-4307

Phone: 1.800.SWEDISH or 206.386.6000

Web: *www.swedish.org*

President: Richard Peterson

Founded: 1910

Description: Founded in 1910, the original Swedish Hospital began as a 24-bed facility in Seattle's First Hill neighborhood. Today, the Swedish/First Hill Campus is a major medical center and the flagship facility for the Swedish health care system.

Swedish Medical Center–Providence

500 - 17th Avenue
Seattle, WA 98122-5711

Phone: 1.800.SWEDISH or 206.320.2000

Web: *www.swedish.org*

President: Richard Peterson

Founded: 2000

Description: Founded by the Sisters of Providence, the hospital that is now Swedish Medical Center/Providence Campus was Seattle's first hospital when it was founded in 1877. In July 2000, Providence Seattle Medical Center, as it was then known, became part of the Swedish health care system. With the addition of the Providence campus, Swedish gained a widely respected heart program, where the Northwest's first open-heart surgery was performed, and the services of highly regarded musculoskeletal specialists.

Swedish National Federation

Susan Johnson
11 Laurelwood Avenue
Leicester, MA 01524

Phone: 508.892.3943

Founded: 1903

Description: To preserve and develop the social and cultural heritage of Sweden.

Activities: Monthly meetings that are held nine times a year, scholarships, midsummer, and other activities.

Swedish Retirement Association

Julie DeCarlo
2320 Pioneer Road
Evanston, IL 60201

Phone: 847.328.8700
Fax: 847.328.8274

E-mail: *swedishretirement.assn@mci2000.com*

Founded: 1899

Description: The Association combines a gracious homelike lifestyle with comprehensive lifelong healthcare services.

Publication: Newsletter, *Tidnings*

 Swedish Roots in Oregon

Stig Annestrand
32461 S.W. Lake Drive
Wilsonville, OR 97070

Phone: 503.694.2382

E-mail: *sundvall@hevanet.com*
Web: *www.sundvall.nu*

President: Stig Annestrand

Description: Swedish Roots in Oregon, an independent non-profit organization which was founded to seek help in answering questions about the Swedes in Oregon—who, where, why, what and how.

Publication: A bi-yearly newsletter

Swedish Ski Club

Winhall Hollow Rd
Bondville, VT 05340

Phone: 802.297.9688

E-mail: *margareta@ugander.com*
Web: *www.swedishskiclub.org*

President: Birgir Nilsen

Founded: 1923/1924 ski season

Description: The purpose of the Club shall be to support and promote skiing in all its forms, recreational and competitive, for all its members, and to endeavor to arrange for a common lodging facility for the members in the Northeastern U.S.

Activities: Participates and organizes ski competitions in New England, as well as being represented in the Vasaloppet in Sweden.

Benefits: Discounted use of facilities

♛ Swedish Society Linnea

Lillian M. Johnson
230 N.E. 56th Avenue
Portland, OR 97213

Phone: 503.236.9281

Chair: Elisabeth Mendenhall

Founded: November 30, 1888

Description: Preserving our Swedish heritage by participate in Swedish activities of our society and other Swedish organizations in the Portland area.

Activities: Participate in an annual Swedish Spring Brunch, Midsummer Festival and Scandinavian Scanfair.

Benefits: Social activities and fraternal fellowship.

Swedish Society of Oakland

Robert J. Thiele
265 Lake Drive
Kensington, CA 94708

Phone: 952.549.3224

President: Anders Lundgren

Founded: March 5, 1901

Activities: Monthly meetings, every second Tuesday, followed
by a social hour.

👑 Swedish Society of San Francisco

Harold Carlson
319 Lunada Court
Los Altos, CA 94022

Phone: 650.941.0348

E-mail: *hcarl@well.com*
Web: *www.swedishamericanhall.com*

Founded: 1873

Description: To foster Scandinavian culture; to provide a meeting place for various Scandinavian organizations including
Oden (Oddfellows), Vasa (Fylgia), Norrlands Clubben, and
the Young Scandinavians.

Activities: Monthly meetings, held every second Tuesday at the Swedish American Hall

♛ Swedish Studies Endowment Program

Carrin Mauritz Patman
University of TX at Austin
2702 Moonlight Bend
Austin, TX 78703

Phone: 512.472.7214

E-mail: *carrinmp@aol.com*
Web: *www.utexas.edu/cola/depts/swedish*

Chair: Kit Belgum

Founded: 1995

Description: The Endowment supports Swedish Studies in the College of Liberal Arts at the University of Texas, Austin, making funds available from time to time for academic programs dealing with all aspects of Swedish culture and civilization, including Swedish science, industry, business, media, language, literature and history, and Sweden in world politics in its relationship to the United States.

♛ Swedish Subcommittee of the Rhode Island Historical Preservation and Heritage Commission

Merlene Mayette
5 Indian Trail South
Wakefield, RI 02879-1914

Phone: 401.783.2242

E-mail: *userm5196159@cs.com*

Chairman: Merlene Mayette

Founded: 1976

Description: Our aim is to keep Swedish traditions and culture alive in the area.

♛ Swedish Texan

Charlene Hanson Jordan
1361 County Road 464
Elgin, TX 78621-5310

Phone: 512.856.2562

E-mail: *charlenehansonjordan@yahoo.com*

♛ Swedish Trade Council

Gudrun Pettersson
150 N. Michigan Avenue, Suite 1200
Chicago, IL 60601

Phone: 312.781.6222 or 1.888 Ask Swed(en)
Fax: 312.346.0683

E-mail: *usa@swedishtrade.se*
Web: *www.swedishtrade.com/usa*

Trade Commissioner: Stefan Bergström

Founded: 1949

Description: The Swedish Trade Council is here to help you do
business with Sweden. With our extensive network and experience in Swedish industry and commerce, we can quickly
identify the right suppliers for you. In addition, we provide
quick, free of charge answers to questions you may have
about Swedish exports. We also work with Swedish companies seeking to establish a presence in the US.

♛ Swedish Travel & Tourism Council

Linda Ericson
655 Third Avenue, 18th Floor
New York, NY 10017-5617

Phone: 212.885.9700
Fax: 212.885.9710

E-mail: *usa@visit-sweden.com*
Web: *www.visit-sweden.com*

Description: The Swedish Travel and Tourism Council is
owned equally by the Swedish state and the Swedish tourist
trade. The Swedish Travel and Tourism Council's mission is
to promote Sweden as a tourist destination.

♛ Swenson Swedish Immigration Research Center

Christina Johansson
Augustana College
639 38th Street
Rock Island, IL 61201

Phone: 309.794.7204
Fax: 309.794.7443

E-mail: *sag@augustana.edu*
Web: *www.augustana.edu/administration/SWENSON*

Director: Dag Blanck

Founded: 1981

Description: The Swenson Center, located at Augustana
College, is a national archive and research institute providing
resources for the study of Swedish immigration to North
America, the communities the immigrants established, and
the role the immigrants and their descendents have played in

American life. This is achieved by promoting and initiating academic research in the field and by collecting and cataloging Swedish-American archival and library materials. Another major role for the Center is to assist people researching their Swedish-American history.

Publications: An annual newsletter, *Swenson Center News,* which is distributed at the end of January each year. *Swedish American Genealogist.*

♛ Swinglish Project

Brian Barnes
P.O. Box 127
Spring Valley, WI 54767

Phone: 715.778.4887

E-mail: *guitart@svtel.net*

Founded: 2000

Description: The Swinglish Project is a joint venture between American jazz guitarist/vocalist Brian Barnes and two Swedish musicians, Hans-Olov Hendrickson (guitar and vocals) and Sven-Bertil Lundström (bass). The group began in the summer of 2000 after a performance tour to Scandinavia introduced Barnes to the jazz repertoire and styling from that part of the world. The songs performed by the great vocalist, Monika Zetterlund figure into the

Swinglish Project repertoire, as well as new interpretations of jazz standards and re-workings of traditional Swedish songs.

 Texas Swedish Pioneers Association

Rod Johnson
P.O. Box 142383
Austin, TX 78714-2383

Phone: 512.869.1851

E-mail: *rodjohnson@thegateway.net*

Founded: 1896

Description: The Association is the only statewide Swedish heritage organization. It strives to bind the Swedes in Texas together to preserve their common heritage.

Publication: A quarterly newsletter on Swedish-Texan heritage

⚜ The Scandinavian Chamber Orchestra of New York

Per Tengstrand
300D South 10th Avenue
Highland Park, NJ 08904

Phone: 732.985.7586
Fax: 732.985.7586

E-mail: *SCOofNYC@aol.com*
Web: *www.mindfeel.com*

Founded: January 2003

Description: To promote Scandinavian music in America, with emphasis on Swedish music.

♛ The Scandinavians, Inc.

Beverly Scherling
P.O. Box 4337
Estes Park, CO 80517

Phone: 970.586.3533

E-mail: *rwsbas@earthlink.net*

Founded: April 7, 1983

Description: To promote and encourage the study and dissemination of information on the cultures of the Scandinavian countries; to meet for fun and fellowship; to further members' knowledge and appreciation of Scandinavian culture.

Activity: Annual Scandinavian Midsummer festival in June.

♛ The Swedish Club

Marv Anderson
241 45th Ave.
Clear Lake, WI 54005

Phone: 715.263.2583
Fax: 715.263.2583

E-mail: *marvdian@spacestar.net*

President: Shawna Gearhart

Founded: Janurary 1, 2003

Description: We are a group of people ranging in age from 25 on up. We all have a common bond of Swedish heritage within us. We meet to learn and discuss customs, geneology, language, make crafts and share stories. We also welcome all who have an interest in Swedish culture, even if you aren't Swedish.

Activities: Christmas party and an Easter Celebration of Traditions in the Spring.

Publications: Newsletter, *Svenska Klubben Nyhete*r and "*Det är nytt för mig*"

Benefits: Meeting other "Swedish" people, developing contacts, geneology, etc., and keeping Swedish culture alive.

♔ Three Crowns American Swedish Association

Shirley Lacher
916 N. 29th St.
Bismarck, ND 58501

Phone: 701.255.4666

Founded: 1980

Description: To promote interest and understanding of the Swedish heritage and culture and to promote fellowship among the members and friendship between the United States and Sweden.

♔ Town of Thorsby

Tracia Bussey
P.O. Box 608
Thorsby, AL 35171

Phone: 205.646.3455
Fax: 205.646.1190

Mayor: Tom Bentley

Founded: 1901

Description: We exist to provide a great place for people to live, work and play with a rich Swedish heritage to enjoy.

Activity: Thorsby Swedish Fest the 3rd Saturday of each September.

♔ Tre Kronor Scandinavian Society

Rose Ann Swanson
P.O. Box 101
Holdrege, NE 68949

Phone: 308.995.6628
Fax: 308.995.9372

Chair: Delores Wendell

Founded: April 10, 1989

Description: A group of persons with Scandinavian heritage who strive to preserve their heritage with programs/events.

Activities: Midsommarfest (Swedish Days), Smorgasbord, Viking Day Dinner and informative meetings, programs, etc.

♔ Twin Cities Nyckelharpalag

Wes Peterson
2907 E. 34th Street
Minneapolis, MN 55406

E-mail: *twincities@nyckelharpa.org*

Founded: 1998

Description: In 1998 four local nyckelharpa players began practicing and playing together. By mid-2001 more than 18 other nyckelharpa and accompanying players joined, making it one of the largest nyckelharpa groups in the US. The group, calling itself the Twin Cities Nyckelharpalag, meets weekly at various members' homes around the Minneapolis/St. Paul area. Their repertoire is drawn from the folk traditions of Uppland, Sweden, where the nyckelharpa tradition has its roots.

Activities: Meets every Tuesday in members' homes.

♛ Twin Cities Swedish Folk Dancers

Kristine Rose
181 Montrose Place
St. Paul, MN 55104

Phone: 651.603.0402
Fax: 651.603.0402

E-mail: *elisepeters@juno.com*

Director: Elise Peters

Founded: 1918

Description: To preserve and promote ethnic Swedish folk dancing through teaching and performances.

Activities: Dance rehearsals, participation in Midsommar celebrations, annual Nordic Ball, Festival of Nations, and sponsorship and/or promotion of workshops in Swedish dance. The dancers will perform for special events by request.

♛ Twin City Dalaföreningen

Janice Lehman
3109 32nd Avenue S.
Minneapolis, MN 55406

Phone: 612.729.8358
Fax: 612.729.0334

Founded: 1947

Description: To meet with people from the province of
Dalarna or anyone else interested in Swedish culture and to
enjoy and preserve the songs, dances, and culture from
Sweden and especially Dalarna.

♛ TystArt, Inc.

Karen Gustafson
1422 Euclid Avenue, Suite 1672
Cleveland, OH 44115

Phone: 216.241.2510
Fax: 216.241.2510

E-mail: *dbenson@lawyersweekly.com*

Founded: December 1, 2003

Description: TystArt is a new kind of arts organization that
explores Scandinavian culture through modern performances

of traditional plays, new theatrical works, film, dance, visual
arts and music.

Uff Da Band

Bruce Muggenburg
2805 Calle Del Rio NW
Albuquerque, NM 87104

Phone: 505.342.0475

E-mail: *bmuggenburg461201@comcast.net*

Founded: 1980

Description: Keeping alive the old time Scandinavian immi-
grant music. Play for different groups/events, mainly the
Scandinavian Club of Albuquerque and the Scandinavian
Dancers of Albuquerque.

Activities: Music in Medicine at the University of New Mexico
hospital venues.

United Swedish Societies

Harry Hedin
1428 Applewood Drive
Freehold, NJ 07728

Phone: 732.431.0841

Founded: 1903

Description: The United Swedish Societies of New York is an umbrella organization for Swedish-American organizations in the metropolitan New York area. The organization's purpose is to achieve closer cooperation among Swedish societies in New York and its surrounding areas on questions and matters which may be of common interest and advantage

Vårblomman

Joy Hamrin
Edgebrook Lutheran Church
5252 W. Devon
Chicago, IL 60646-4145

Phone: 773.777.5096

E-mail: *varblomman@hotmail.com*
Web: *www.varblomman.org*

Description: Vårblomman is a very active Children's Club performing all over the Chicagoland area. Vårblomman was founded by Swedish immigrants desiring to preserve their heritage. The club works to maintain the Swedish culture in America through teaching the youth the Swedish language, songs and folk dances. Through these measures, the main goal can be achieved, that of continuing the time-honored Swedish traditions to the next generation.

Activities: Meetings every 2nd and 4th Saturday; sponsors many fundraising pancake breakfasts, performs annually at the Museum of Science and Industry's Christmas Around the World, the Botanic Garden's Swedish Festival and many other festivities.

Benefits: Scholarships to the Concordia College International Language Summer Camp in Minnesota

♛ Värmlands Förbundet

Dwight Gunberg
3407 62nd Avenue N
Minneapolis, MN 55429

Phone: 763.561.2027

E-mail: *swedenhall@aol.com*

Founded: 1927

Description: To preserve Swedish heritage and in particular to maintain significant connections with Värmland; to provide the opportunity for those with these interests to socialize.

♛ Värmlands-Vännerna

Alvalene Karlsson
1844 Second Avenue
New York, NY 10028

Phone: 212.426.1376

E-mail: *apKarlsson@aol.com*

Founded: 1971

Description: To preserve the culture of Värmland in the United States and to support the Emigrant Register in Karlstad, Sweden

Vasa Folk Dancers of New York

Jeanne Eriksson Widman
P.O. Box 0712
Baldwin, NY 11510

Phone: 718.415.0602

E-mail: *jeannewidman@aol.com*

President: Jeanne Eriksson Widman

Founded: 1950

Description: To preserve the traditional Swedish folk dances, ring dances, bygdedans and gammaldans.

Activities: Rehearsals two times per month, performances at many festivals and special occasions, including Sweden Day, Scandinavian Night, Scandinavian Fest, and the annual Scandinavian Christmas Ball and Luciafest; hosting of visitors, folkdancers, and musicians. The dancers performed for King Carl XVI Gustaf and Queen Silvia in 1988.

Vasa Jr. Folk Dancers

Janice Lehman
3109 32nd Ave. S
Minneapolis, MN 55406

Phone: 612.729.0334

 Vasa Museum

Grace Nelson
29699 Småland Road
Welch, MN 55089

 Västergötland Society

Mel Lijsing
4501 Shoreline Dr. #229
Spring Park, MN 55384

Phone: 952.471.4082

President: Marilyn Braun

Re-organized in September 1990 by Rev. Clifford Anderson
after being dormant since the mid 1960s

Description: To promote awareness of roots in Västergötland
and to provide contact with others with similar roots; to promote appreciation of the Swedish language, heritage and cul-

ture; to strengthen ties with Sweden; to provide fellowship; assistance with family history; and Swedish entertainment.

Activities: Five yearly meetings at the American Swedish Institute, a picnic and a meeting at the annual Svenskarnas Dag.

Publication: Newsletter printed seven times per year

Vesterheim Norwegian-American Museum

523 West Walter Street
P.O. Box 379
Decorah, IA 52101

Phone: 563.382.9681
Fax: 563.382.8828

E-mail: *vesterheim@vesterheim.org*
Web: *www.vesterheim.org/index.htm*

President: Dr. E.J. Norby

Founded: 1877

Description: Vesterheim is a center for the preservation, interpretation and study of material relating to the life and culture of Norwegian-Americans. As such it instills in Americans of all ethnic backgrounds an awareness of the great diversity in their cultural heritage and enables Norwegian Americans to see, to understand, and to appreciate their place in the mosaic of American culture.

Activities: Holds National juried exhibitions in traditional knife making, rosemaling, rug hooking, weaving and wood-carving. Sponsored by First State Bank, held every year at the Nordic Fest. Open every day of the year except for major holidays. Group rates and specialty tours can be arranged and a teacher's guide is available.

Publications: Quarterly Vesterheim Rosemaling letter and catalog.

Benefits: Member publications; 10% discount on Museum-butik items, free admissions to museum, notice of classes, new exhibits, specialty items.

Vestgota Gille of Chicago

Urban Leo
Svithiod Hall
5516 West Lawrence Avenue
Chicago, IL 60630

President: Sten Bjorkling

Founded: January 3, 1902

Description: To unite men born in the province of Västergötland, Sweden, and their male offspring; to revive memories of their birthplace and forefathers' virtues.

Activities: Monthly meetings, annual herring breakfast and an annual Christmas party.

♛ Viking Age Club

Dennis Rusinko
617 24th Avenue NE
Minneapolis, MN 55418

Phone: 612.789.2272

E-mail: *rusinkodennis@hotmail.com*
Web: *www.vikingage.com/vac/vac.html*

Founders: Gary Anderson and Dennis Rusinko

Founded: 1985

Description: The Viking Age Club-Sons of Norway was
formed to study the history of the Vikings and to lecture to
the public about the true facts of this era. The Viking Age
Club-Sons of Norway is a non-profit educational organization based out of Sons of Norway Lodge #1-517. No paid
employees of any kind, an all volunteer labor force making
buying the items that the club owns. Today the club is made
up of people from all walks of life with memberships all over
the United States and Canada.

Viking Workshop

David Peterson
18514 Hawks Hill Road
Wildwood, MO 63069

Phone: 636.458.4872

E-mail: *dwpete26@juno.com*

Founded: September 2002

Description: The Viking Workshop is a study group composed
mostly of members of the three St. Louis area Scandinavian
clubs: The Swedish Council, Den Danske Klub and the
Norwegian Society of St. Louis, but anyone interested in
Viking lore is welcome. Each month we choose some aspect
of Viking lore to study—such as trade routes, ship building,
religion, art, etc. We each study what material we can find
on that topic, in books, magazines, and on the internet, to
discuss what we have learned at the next meeting.

Activities: The group meets from 1:00 to 3:00 pm on the
fourth Tuesday of the month at the Kirkwood, MO Public
Library.

Vikingland American Scandinavian Organization

Elda Lindquist
6800 North Lake Mina Road NW
Alexandria, MN 56508

Phone: 320.763.7478

President: Ray Englund

Founded: March 27, 1980

Description: To keep in touch with Swedish heritage and to
encourage travel to Sweden or other countries.

Activities: Quarterly meetings, Walpurgis Night, winter smörgåsbord, Midsummer Fest and Flag raising.

Publication: Quarterly newsletter, *Swede Talk*

♛ Vikingship Restoration Committee

Carl R. Hansen
800 E. Northwest Hwy., Suite 202
Mt. Prospect, IL 60056

Phone: 847.818.1515
Fax: 847.818.1580

Commissioner: Carl R. Hansen

Founded: November 28, 1979

Description: To provide a permanent location for the Chicago Park District Viking Ship; to restore the ship and create an educational museum type exhibit.

Activities: Various meetings.

Benefits: Permanent preservation and exhibition of the Viking Ship.

♛ VocalEssence

Katryn Conlin
1900 Nicollet Avenue
Minneapolis, MN 55403

Phone: 612.547.1451
Fax: 612.547.1484

E-mail: *info@vocalessence.org*
Web: *www.vocalessence.org*

Founder and Artistic Director: Philip Brunelle

Founded: 1969

Description: For over 3 decades, VocalEssence has been revered
in Minneapolis and around the world as a premier producer
of innovate choral music experiences. VocalEssence explores
the realm of great choral music—music that stirs the soul.
From a cappella to symphonic, from spoken work to the
voices of a massed chorus, there is no other organization
quite like VocalEssence in its range, variety and quality of
performance.

Publication: Quarterly newsletter

Walter Eriksson Musikfest-Skandjam

Jeanne Eriksson Widman
Skandjam
119 Creek Road
Andover, NJ 07822

Phone: 973.786.6398 (tickets)

E-mail: *skandjam@skandjam.com*
Web: *www.skandjam.com/index/html*

President: Jeanne Eriksson Widman

Founded: 1994

Description: This festival began in order to commemorate the
life and talent of the great Scandinavian accordionist, Walter
Eriksson. It seeks to bring together as many talented musicians as possible for a two-day festival in the Northwest hills
of New Jersey—at Vasa Park near Budd Lake.

Activities: The festival takes place for the two days during the
Memorial Day weekend. This year is the tenth anniversary.
Also offers workshops in fiddle, adult and children's folk
dancing and accordion; sponsor scholarships for deserving
music students; sponsored the opening of the Museum at the
Swedish Home on Staten Island.

♛ West Shore Scandinavian Society

Pat Thomas
211 Hughes Street
Manistee, MI 49660-1221

Founded: January 16, 1983

Description: To preserve, promote and publicize the culture, heritage, and traditions of the Scandinavian countries; to provide fellowship among the members.

Publication: A cookbook, *How We Cook Scandinavian: Recipes and Memories,* 1993

Young Scandinavian's Club

Renee Hersson
P.O. Box 640610
San Francisco, CA 94164-0601

Phone: 415.346.7450

Web: *www.ysc.org*

President: Stig A. Tisell

Founded: August 19, 1950

Description: A Bay Area social club for singles and families with ties to the Scandinavian countries. We meet in a cabin at Clear Lake, as well as a cabin on Lake Tahoe.

Activities: Water-ski, hike, sail, bike, sauna/roll in snow, ski, sunbathe, climb mountains, dance, swim, eat, drink, party.

Publication: Monthly newsletter

Benefits: Calendar of monthly activities, newsletter, access to Clear Lake and Lake Tahoe.

Zaida Singers

Zaida Hansson Binetti
P.O. Box 2142
Los Gatos, CA 95031-2142

Phone: 408.335.5963
Fax: 408.335.1808

E-mail: *zaida811@cs.com*

President: Zaida Hansson Binetti

Founded: 1975

Activities: Weekly rehearsals, plus: five to six Lucia performances, Midsommar, SVEADAL; and for the Swedish service at the Norwegian Seaman's church, as well as other churches in the area.

National Organizations

A number of agencies and organizations include multiple chapters in the United States, Canada and Sweden. These national organizations focus their efforts in the preservation and promotion of Sweden and the Swedish heritage in a specific category such as business or music.

The organizations and institutions in this section include: The Vasa Order of America (VOA), Swedish American Chambers of Commerce (SACC), Swedish Women's Educational Association (SWEA), American Union of Swedish Singers (A.U.S.S.), Independent Order of Svithiod (IOS), Independent Order of Vikings (IOV), and the American-Scandinavian Foundation (ASF).

 indicates the organization is an affiliate of the Swedish Council of America

AMERICAN SCANDINAVIAN FOUNDATION

👑 American Scandinavian Foundation

Scandinavia House
58 Park Avenue
New York, NY 10016

Phone: 212.879.9779

E-mail: *info@amscan.org*
Web: *www.amscan.org*

Founded: 1910

Description: The American Scandinavian Foundation promotes international understanding through educational and cultural exchange between the United States and Denmark, Finland, Iceland, Norway and Sweden.

Activities: The organization supports a variety of activities and programs, such as fellowships, grants, trainee placement, publishing, membership offerings, and cultural activities.

Publications: Magazine: *Scandinavian Review.* Newsletter: *Scan.* Annual Newsletter: *The Longboat*

Benefits: Members receive a variety of benefits, depending on the level of financial commitment, such as an advance notice of films, lectures and concerts; volunteer opportunities, subscription to the *Scandinavian Review*, discount at the online store, and passes to ASF events.

♛ American Scandinavian Association at Augustana College

Loryann Eis
2037 15th St.
Moline, IL 61265

Phone: 309.762.8303
Fax: 309.762.8303

E-mail: *leis@derbytech.com*
Web: *www.augustana.edu/administration/swenson/asa*

President: John E. Norton

Founded: 1934

Description: To stimulate and promote interest in relations and culture between America and all five of the Nordic countries. To preserve the Nordic heritage in western Illinois and eastern Iowa. To advance Nordic culture in the United States, and United States culture in the Nordic countries.

Activities: Some activities include: Midsommar Fest, Kräftskiva, Lucia fest in association with Augustana College's Scandinavian Department, annual Pea Soup Supper, Bus trips to Andersonville and IKEA.

Publication: A periodic newsletter

Benefits: Opportunities to participate in ASA activities, informational newsletters, discounts on ASA trips, and occasional cooking demonstrations.

American Scandinavian Association of Illinois

Carol Beu
2821 W. Rascher Ave.
Chicago, IL 60625

Phone: 773.878.0312

♛ American Scandinavian Association of the Great Plains

A. John Pearson
P.O. Box 2765
Lindsborg, KS 67456

Phone: 785.227.2302

E-mail: *pearson@informatics.net*

President: DeVere Blomberg

Founded: October, 12 1973

Description: To promote and strengthen the cultural, educational and intellectual relations between the organization's region in the United States and the countries of Denmark, Finland, Iceland, Norway, and Sweden; to preserve the Scandinavian-American heritage; to encourage the continued recognition and observation of Scandinavian customs and folklore; to sponsor and promote contemporary activities, concerts, and events to that end.

Activities: Meetings held approximately once every two months and help with Svensk Hyllningsfest.

Publication: *American Scandinavian Association of the Great Plains*

Benefits: Subscription to *Nordic Reach* magazine and scholarships.

American Scandinavian Association of the National Capital Area, Inc.

Bernice W. Munsey
3623 N. 37th St.
Arlington, VA 22207

Phone: 703.276.8228

Web: *www.geocities.com/asanca.geo/*

Founded: 1963

Description: The American Scandinavian Association (ASA) is a local non-profit cultural organization incorporated in the District of Columbia. The goals of ASA are: to promote cultural exchange between the United States and the Nordic Countries of Denmark, Finland, Iceland, Norway & Sweden; to increase understanding of the Nordic peoples and societies among Americans; and to provide a forum where people interested in Scandinavia can meet and enjoy Nordic culture and activities.

Activities: Monthly meetings (September–May), on the third
Monday of the month at St. John's Church in Bethesda,
MD.

Publication: Monthly newsletter

Benefits: Monthly meetings with social entertainment and cultural activities, monthly newsletter, grants & scholarships,
and ASA's Scandinavian Literature Group.

American Scandinavian Council

Carol Schrader
1551 Ashland, Suite 409
Des Plaines, IL 60016

Phone: 847.635.1199

American Scandinavian Foundation of Los Angeles

James Koenig
P.O. Box 292329
Los Angeles, CA 90029

Phone: 231.661.4273

American Scandinavian Foundation of San Francisco Bay Area Associates

Barbara Erickson
265 Fowler Avenue
San Francisco, CA 94127

Phone: 415.661.9385

American Scandinavian Foundation of Santa Barbara

Ted Gloger
P.O. Box 4065
Santa Barbara, CA 93140

♛ American Scandinavian Foundation of Thousand Oaks

Howard Rockstad
1227 Tierra Dr.
Thousand Oaks, CA 91362

Phone: 805.497.3717

Description: To preserve and celebrate Scandinavian heritage.

American Scandinavian Society of New York, Inc.

Pertti J. Ripatti
317 E. 52nd St.
New York, NY 10022

Phone: 212.751.0714

American Scandinavians of Monterey Central Coast

Kjell Fongstad
P.O. Box 1081
Monterey, CA 93940

Phone: 831.372.4083

ASFTA (American-Scandinavian Foundation Texas Associates)

Nikolas White
P.O. Box 5033
Austin, TX 78763

E-mail: *nik@triand.com*
Web: *www.asfta.org*

♛ Central Iowa Associates of the American-Scandinavian Foundation

Charles Farr
740 16th Street
Des Moines, IA 50314-1601

Phone: 515-255-1340

E-mail: *farrch@mchsi.com*

President: Charles E. Farr

Founded: 1975

Description: Educate, primarily on Scandinavia.

Activities: Monthly meetings, Santa Lucia and Traditional meals.

Publication: Newsletter

♛ Friends of Scandinavia

Jim Wilson
6400 Lasalle Lane
Raleigh, NC 27612

Phone: 919.847.5599

E-mail: *jim-wilson@mindspring.com*
Web: *www.rtnet.org/~nordic*

President: Jan Fagerberg

Founded: October 1979

Description: To provide activities and programs that broaden knowledge, understanding, and appreciation of Scandinavian culture; to preserve and keep alive the traditions of Scandinavia; to foster fellowship and friendship among persons of Scandinavian heritage and those interested in that heritage.

Activities: Meetings on the third Sunday of each month (Sept. –June), St. Lucia, lutfisk dinners and a midsommar celebration.

Publication: A monthly newsletter, *FOS News*—available online

Minnesota Associates of the American-Scandinavian Foundation

Elaine Grahm
2032 Kentucky Avenue South
St. Louis Park, MN 55426

Phone: 612.545.7669

 Northwest Iowa Associates of ASF

Raymond Anderson
713 Johnson Street
Alta, IA 51002

Phone: 712.200.2050

Founded: 1971

Description: To preserve and promote Scandinavian traditions, culture and customs.

♛ Scandinavian American Foundation of Georgia

Margareta Martin
P.O. Box 1166
Decatur, GA 30031

Phone: 404.373.9919

E-mail: *info@scandga.org*
Web: *www.scandga.org/Foundation*

Chairman: Jorgen P. Conradsen

Founded: March 3, 1983

Description: The Scandinavian American Foundation of Georgia is a non-profit organization dedicated to the exchange of educational, cultural, and amateur athletic endeavors between the countries of Denmark, Finland, Iceland, Norway, Sweden and the State of Georgia. Founded in 1983, the Foundation has channeled the resources of individuals, corporations, organizations and government agencies in achieving these goals.

Publication: A quarterly newsletter: *Insights*

♔ Scandinavian Heritage Foundation

Priscilla Blumel
1521 S.W. Marlow Ave.
Suite C
Portland, OR 97225-5101

Phone: 503.296.0842
Fax: 503.297.5882

E-mail: *shf@mindspring.com*
Web: *www.scanheritage.org*

President: Kristine Olson

Founded: 1986

Description: The Scandinavian Heritage Foundation's goal is to preserve, communicate and celebrate Scandinavian heritage and culture.

Activities: Scanfeast, ScanFair, Cook n' Eat, Friday Night Lecture Series at Portland State University, Annual Meeting, August Crawfish Festival, Genealogical class series and Scan Sampler at Portland State University.

Publication: Quarterly Newsletter: *SHF, Scandinavian Heritage Foundation*

Scandinavian Society of Cincinnati

Birgit Jorgensen
1287 Jeremy Court
Cincinnati, OH 45240

Phone: 513.825.9358 or 513.333.2987

Web: *www.geocities.com/scansoccinci*

President: Birgit Jorgensen

Founded: June 7, 1963

Description: The Scandinavian Society of Cincinnati is an organization to promote appreciation and understanding of Scandinavian heritage and culture amongst native-born Scandinavians, persons of Scandinavian lineage, and friends of Scandinavia.

Activities: Holding regular dinner and other meetings to celebrate the traditional Scandinavian holidays and events, smorgasbords, entertainment at our meetings and elsewhere, sponsoring a Scandinavian folk dance group, and donating funds for cultural and educational activities.

Publication: Newsletter

Southern Florida Associates of the American Scandinavian Foundation

Helen Meyer
8305 Sunrise Lakes Blvd.
Fort Lauderdale, FL 33422

Phone: 305.742.8062

Western Carolinas Associates of ASF

Eiler R. Cook
1021 Saddlebrook Dr.
Hendersonville, NC 29793

Phone: 828.692.0323
Fax: 828.692.0600

Web: *biteiler@bellsouth.net*

President: Eiler R. Cook

Founded: March 1982

Description: Our membership consists of those interested in Scandinavia or of Scandinavian background. Social get-togethers and fundraising for local education projects in North and South Carolina.

Activities: Spring and Fall dinners, Scandinavian picnic and attendance at Brevard Music Center musical or operetta, booth at annual N.C. Apple Festival in Hendersonville, and a "Lucia" Christmas program.

Publication: Periodic newsletter before each event.

Benefits: Exposure to periodic Scandinavian cultural events and select subscriptions to *Nordic Reach* and *Scandinavian Review.*

AMERICAN UNION OF SWEDISH SINGERS—A.U.S.S.

♕ American Union of Swedish Singers

Jody Jones
25505 N.W. Svea Drive
Hillsboro, OR 97124

Phone: 503.647.5147

E-mail: *traffcon@earthlink.net*
Web: *ourworld.cs.com/auss1892*

President: Jody Jones

Founded: 1892

Description: The objectives of the A.U.S.S. are to promote and perpetuate Swedish chorus singing and knowledge of Swedish songs, cultivate an appreciation of Swedish music, and work for unity and cooperation between Swedish choruses in the United States and Canada.

Activities: Every four years the A.U.S.S. holds a national convention. This is a chance for singers with a common interest to get together and share ideas, songs and fellowship.

Publication: Quarterly newsletter: *Musiktidning*

♛ A.U.S.S. Cultural Heritage Foundation

Walter Carlson
14400 Kandi Ct.
Indian Rocks Beach, FL 34615

Phone: 727.596.4314

Web: *www.ourworld.cs.com/auss1892/whatis.htm*

Founded: November 1892

Description: Founded to preserve the history of the A.U.S.S. by collecting and housing the organization's memorabilia. The foundation maintains a room at the Midway Village Museum in Rockford, Illinois, where you can view old photographs and uniforms, memorabilia from past conventions and listen to tapes.

Publication: A book, *A Century of Song*, published in 1992

Apollo Singing Society (men's chorus)

Hamden, CT

♕ Arpi Swedish Male Chorus of Metropolitan Detroit

Bengt Brogren
Swedish Club
22398 Ruth Street
Farmington Hills, MI 48336-4249

Phone: 248.553.4593

E-mail: *bengtb@msn.com*
Web: *www.swedishclub.net*

Director: Arthur Elander

Founded: 1932

Description: Organized in the 1930s, it was the forerunner, nucleus and organizer of the Swedish Club (of greater Detroit) and now continues as an integral part of the Swedish Club. It is dedicated to the preservation of Swedish & Scandinavian ethnicity through music & often time entertains at the Club and public events and through its A.U.S.S. association with some 24 choruses throughout the country. It uses its talents to "reach out" nationwide.

Activities: Annual Lucia, midsommar, fundraisers and multiple concerts.

Publication: Bi-monthly newsletter

♛ ASI Male Chorus

Gunnar Wikstrom
6035 Gardena Lane NE
Fridley, MN 55432

Phone: 763.571.9632

E-mail: *gunnarwik@aol.com*

President: Gunnar Wikstrom

Founded: 1936

Description: Dedicated to preserving the Swedish culture through song and the preservation of Swedish music.

Activities: 2 Frukosts at the ASI, Spring concert, Sångarfest, Lucia, Midsommar and a Christmas Fair.

Publication: Monthly newsletter: *ASI Male Chorus Update*

Chicago Swedish Glee Club (men's chorus)

Chicago, IL

Chicago Swedish Male Chorus

Chicago, IL

Dam Kören (women's chorus)

Jamestown, NY

♛ Flickorna Fem

Carline Bengtsson
111 E. Kellogg Blvd
St. Paul, MN 55101

Phone: 651.222.8626
Fax: 651.292.8341

Web: *www.flickornafem.com*

Founded: June 1997

Description: Sharing traditional, Swedish music and traditions within the American-Scandinavian community.

Publications: 2 CDs: *Summer Songs* (1999) and *Love Songs* (2001)

North Star Singers (men's chorus)

Fairfield, CT

Northern Lights Singers (women's chorus)

Fairfield, CT

Scandia Ladies Chorus

Portland, OR

♛ Scandia Women's Chorus

Lillian Lagerkvist
17994 Crystal River Dr.
Macomb, MI 48042

Phone: 586.786.6368

Web: *www.swedishclub.net/newspage1.htm*

Description: The chorus, of approximately 40+ women, sing not only in Swedish and English, but songs of all the Scandinavian countries. Although several singers were born in Sweden, most of the members do not speak fluent Swedish.

Scandinavian Chorus of Milwaukee (mixed chorus)

Milwaukee, WI

Scandinavian Chorus of Portland (men's chorus)

Portland, OR

Scandinavian Women's Chorus of Connecticut

Hamden, CT

Scandinavian Women's Chorus of Rhode Island

Providence, RI

Skandia/Orphei Drängar (mixed chorus)

Springfield, MA

St. Paul Swedish Male Chorus

St. Paul, MN

Stämbandet (mixed chorus)

Boston, MA

Suncoast Swedish Veterans (men's chorus)

St. Petersburg, FL

Svea Male Chorus

Seattle, WA

Svea Söner Singing Society (men's chorus)

Rockford, IL

Swedish Glee Club (men's chorus)

Waukegan, IL

Swedish Museum Singers (mixed chorus)

Philadelphia, PA

Swedish Women's Chorus, Seattle

Seattle, WA

Vasa Voices (mixed chorus)

Cleveland, OH

Verdandi Male Chorus

Providence, RI

♕ Viking Male Chorus

Ronald Stenstrom
110 W. 3rd Street, Apt. 601
Jamestown, NY 14701-5119

Phone: 716.484.2183

E-mail: *ronaldstenstrom@webtv.net*

INDEPENDENT ORDER OF SVITHIOD

Independent Order of Svithiod

Betty Jane Clausen
5518 W. Lawrence Avenue
Chicago, IL 60630-3493

Phone: 773.736.1191

E-mail: *iosvithiod@juno.com*
Web: *http://hometown.aol.com/scanold*

President: Gerald Schubring

Founded: December 3, 1880

Description: A Scandinavian fraternal organization, composed of eleven subordinate lodges throughout Illinois, which promote Scandinavian culture and heritage through social activities

Activities: Annual Spring Frolic; Smörgåsbord dinners; dances; annual Svithiod bowling meet; St. Lucia Day; sponsorship of a children's singing and dancing group known as Sverige-Barnen; sponsorship of the Svithiod Scholarship Fund and Svithiod Benevolent Assistance Program Fund

Publication: A monthly newsletter: *Svithiod Journal*

Benefits: Svithiod preserves the Scandinavian heritage and culture of its members. Svithiod offers charitable and educational programs for the benefit of its members through the Benevolent Assistance Program and the Scholarship Fund.

Svithiod offers ritualistic activities through meetings of the Grand Lodge and subordinate lodges. Svithiod offers social programs such as dinners, dances, picnics, card parties, theater parties and culturally oriented activities. Svithiod offers sport activities. Members are eligible to participate in bowling meets and golf outings. Svithiod provides a monthly publication, the Svithiod Journal, which has kept members informed of news and activities within local lodges and the Grand Lodge since 1898.

IOS, Andree Lodge #19

Chicago, IL

IOS, Astrid Lodge #65

Chicago, IL

 IOS, Brage Lodge #29

Luan Borquist, Recording Secretary
1435 E. Fairoaks Avenue
Peoria, IL 61603-1669

Phone: 309.685.6756

IOS, Corona/John Ericsson Lodge #23

Rockford, IL

IOS, Frej Lodge #16

Moline, IL

IOS, Linden Park Lodge #15

Chicago, IL

IOS, Orion Lodge #64

Franklin Park, IL

IOS, Sten Sture Lodge #32

Melrose Park, IL

 IOS, Svithiod Lodge #1

Edmund Baumann
5516 W. Lawrence Avenue
Chicago, IL 60630

Phone: 773.338.2895

E-mail: *edmund6014@aol.com*

IOS, Vasa Lodge #17

Galesburg, IL

IOS, Verdandi Lodge #3

Chicago, IL

INDEPENDENT ORDER OF VIKINGS

Independent Order of Vikings

Joyce Copp
5250 S. 6th St.
P.O. Box 5147
Springfield, IL 62705-5147

Phone: 877.241.6006

E-mail: *member_services@iovikings.org*
Web: *www.iovikings.org*

Grand Chief: Raymond P. Knutson

Founded: 1890

Description: The Independent Order of Vikings is a fraternal benefit society often called the IOV. As a fraternal benefit society, we provide cultural and financial benefits to our members. Our organization was founded over 100 years ago and has grown to encompass many subordinate lodges throughout the US. Our Scandinavian founders endeavored to retain the Scandinavian traditions of the past as the spirit of forming the IOV. Our goals then were the same as they are now: Unity of fellowship, help in time of need, and a sound investment in the future.

Activities: Many activities are available for participant members including, but not limited to, putting on dinners or parties, holding Scandinavian instruction, dances, smorgasbords,

herring breakfasts, junior clubs, bowling, golf, boating, initi-
ation and drill teams, etc.

Publication: A quarterly publication: *The Viking Journal,
Vikingen*

Benefits: IOV life insurance, discount prescription card, scholarships, etc.

IOV, Baltic Lodge #56

Rockford, IL

IOV, Baltic Star Lodge #112

Rockford, IL

IOV, Brage Lodge #2

Chicago, IL

IOV, Clara Lodge #118

Moline, IL

IOV, Drake Lodge #3

Chicago, IL

IOV, Edmund Lodge #91

Woburn, MA

👑 IOV, Ellida Lodge #25

Raymond Knutson
1111 5th Avenue
Rockford, IL 61104

Phone: 815.393.4926

IOV, Gripsholm Lodge #83

Lynn, MA

IOV, Harald Lodge #13

Tinley Park, IL

IOV, Idun Lodge #58

Grand Rapids, MI

♛ IOV, Ingjald Lodge #65

318 Washington St.
Jamestown, NY 14701

Phone: 716.487.9305

IOV, Linne Lodge #57

Muskegon, MI

IOV, Lodbrok Lodge#47

Lake Forest, IL

IOV, Manhem Lodge #37

Highland Park, IL

IOV, Mimer Lodge #33

Geneva, IL

IOV, Neptun Lodge #35

St. Charles, IL

IOV, Orvar Odd Lodge #24

Omaha, NE

IOV, Ring Lodge #18

Batavia, IL 60510

IOV, Sigurd Lodge #30

Kenosha, WI

♛ IOV, Skandia Lodge #68

Andrea Tolonen
2877 S.E. Franklin
Portland, OR 97202

Phone: 503.236.1734

Chief: Bruce Tolonen

Founded: 1927

Description: Our main goal is to have fun, learn about Swedish culture, explore our past, participate in Scandinavian community activities, and to keep this old organization alive.

Activities: Swedish brunch, wife-carrying contest at Midsommar Festival, Booth at ScanFair in December and a Christmas Dinner.

Benefits: Fun, culture, lunches out (restaurants), field trips to visit Scandinavian places, friendship.

IOV, Sleipner Lodge #96

Bergenfield, NJ

IOV, Starke Lodge #42

Oakland, NE

IOV, Stenkil Lodge #92

Braintree, MA

IOV, Thor Lodge #9

Moline, IL

IOV, Thorbjorn #40

Berwyn, IL

IOV, Thule Lodge #72

Buffalo, NY

IOV, Trotsig Lodge #99

Summit, NJ

IOV, Waldemar Lodge #88

Concord, NH

SWEDISH AMERICAN CHAMBER OF COMMERCE—SACC

 SACC–USA

Gunilla Girardo
1403 King Street
Alexandria, VA 22314

Phone: 703.836.6560
Fax: 703.836.6561

E-mail: *admin@sacc-usa.org*
Web: *www.sacc-usa.org*

Chairman: Anders Berggren; **President:** Gunilla Girardo

Founded: 1906

Description: SACC–USA is a national organization for the regional Swedish-American Chambers of Commerce located all over the U.S., as well as companies and corporations in Sweden.

Activities: Annual Entrepreneurial Days—linking Swedish and U.S. businesses and providing a forum for exchange of information and networking

Publications: *Currents*, SACC–USA's magazine (five issues/year) reaching a key readership of decision makers in Sweden and the U.S. This is an excellent tool for members and Chambers to promote their products and services.

Publishing an annual *SACC–USA Membership Directory*, an essential resource for networking and business contacts.

Benefits: Providing access to a valuable network of 18 regional Chambers in the U.S. and Swedish corporate members.

SACC Chambers provide a broad range of services including: market research, partner and distribution searches, seminars, expert advice, and much more.

Organizing annual Entrepreneurial Days—linking Swedish and U.S. businesses and providing a forum for exchange of information and networking.

SACC, Arizona

Mesa, AZ

 SACC, Atlanta

Morgan Cederblom
4775 Peachtree Industrial Blvd.
Bldg 300, Suite 300
Norcross, GA 30092

Phone: 770.670.2500

E-mail: *sacc@sacc-atlanta.org*
Web: *www.sacc-atlanta.org*

SACC, Carolinas

Raleigh, NC

 SACC, Chicago

Jim Runnfeldt
150 N. Michigan Ave., #1200
Chicago, IL 60601-7594

Phone: 312.781.6234

Web: *www.sacc-usa.org/chicago/index*

👑 SACC, Colorado

Roland Nilsson
13558 W. Alaska Dr.
Lakewood, CO 80228

Phone: 303.985.3538

E-mail: *Ekenskis@aol.com*
Web: *www.sacc-usa.org/colorado*

♛ SACC, Detroit

Melissa Mark, Executive Director
P.O. Box 396
Birmingham, MI 48012-0396

Phone: 248.644.8170

E-mail: *sacc-detroit@prodigy.net*
Web: *www.sacc-detroit.org*

Chair: Stieg Ingvarsson, **President:** Frank Wennberg

Founded: 1988

Description: Our primary mission is to enhance trade, commerce and investment between the Detroit region and Sweden.

Activities: Pub nights, networking fair, golf tournament, picnic, crayfish party and Jul luncheon.

SACC, Florida

Miami, FL

♔ SACC, Greater Los Angeles

Erik Nord
10940 Wilshire Blvd.
Suite #700
Los Angeles, CA 90024

Phone: 818.761.1034

E-mail: *info@sacc-gla.org*
Web: *www.sacc-gla.org*

♔ SACC, Minnesota

Peter Hedström
2600 Park Avenue
Minneapolis, MN 55407

Phone: 612-991-3001

E-mail: *info@sacc-minnesota.org*
Web: *www.sacc-minnesota.org*

SACC, New England

Weston, MA

SACC, New York

New York, NY

SACC, Philadelphia

780 Third Avenue
King of Prussia, PA 19406

Phone: 610.265.1939

E-mail: *information@sacc-philadelphia.org*
Web: *www.sacc-philadelphia.org*

President: Urban Svensson

Founded: 1999

Description: To develop strong Swedish-American business relations and foster better understanding of the cultural differences in business in the Pennsylvania, southern New Jersey and Delaware region.

Activities: Monthly networking opportunities, regular corporate presentations and events.

Publications: Newsletter: *SACC Philly Update* and and email: *SACC Philadelphia E-News*

Benefits: Free subscription to *Currents* (SACC–USA's magazine), monthly networking opportunities, free subscription to the local newsletter, a personal copy of the regional membership directory, and access to SACC–USA's network of more than 2000 members in 18 chapters.

SACC, San Diego, Tijuana

San Diego, CA

 SACC, San Francisco

Mark Bünger
564 Market St. #305
San Francisco, CA 94104

Phone: 415.781.4189

E-mail: *info@sacc-sf.org*
Web: *www.sacc-usa.org/sf*

SACC, Seattle

Seattle, WA

 SACC, Texas

Astrid Marklund
P.O. Box 591366
Houston, TX 77259-1366

Phone: 281.461.6215
Fax: 281.461.6216

E-mail: *astrid@asmdevelopment.com*
Web: *www.sacctx.com*

SACC, Utah

Salt Lake City, UT

SACC, Washington DC

Eva Ohlin
1501 M. Street NW
Washington, DC 20005

Phone: 202.467.2648

Web: *www.sacc-dc.org*

Description: Anyone interested in Swedish-American business and trade.

Activities: Meet during luncheons, seminars, business clubs.

SWEDISH WOMEN'S EDUCATIONAL ASSOCIATION— SWEA

♛ SWEA International Inc.

Boel Alkdal, Administrator
5928 Balfour Court Suite B
Carlsbad, CA 92008

Phone: 760.918.9653
Fax: 760.918.9654

E-mail: *office@swea.org*
Web: *www.swea.org*

President: Christina Moliteus, **Founder:** Agneta Nilsson

Founded: November 1979

Description: SWEA, Swedish Women's Educational Association Inc., is a global non-profit organization for Swedish-speaking women who live or have lived abroad.

Activities: We gather to enjoy our Swedish language, background and culture. SWEA is both a meeting point and a safety net with links all over the world, making life abroad easier, providing support when arriving in a new place or when returning to the home land.

SWEA's objective is to protect the Swedish language, support and inform about our culture and traditions. Also SWEA will act as an intermediary in supplying personal and professional contacts and establish a network for its members throughout the world.

SWEA supports education through scholarships and various projects with a Swedish connection.

International conference every other year for all chapters, lunches and dinners during the summer months in Sweden. Each chapter has its own activities which vary from chapter to chapter.

Publication: Bi-annual membership magazine: *SWEA Forum*

Benefits: Health insurance, discounts for car rentals, subscriptions to certain magazines and membership in certain organizations.

 SWEA, Arizona

Suzanne Becker
14013 N. 61st Place
Scottsdale, AZ 88254

Phone: 480.948.5917

E-mail: *arizona@swea.org*
Web: *www.swea.org*

SWEA, Atlanta

Monica Eklund
4344 Highborne Dr. NE
Marietta, GA 30066

Phone: 770.578.4698

E-mail: *atlanta@swea.org*
Web: *www.swea.org*

👑 **SWEA, Boston**

Åsa Eldh
15 Lincoln Rd.
Wellesley, MA 02481

Phone: 781.237.4079
Fax: 781.235.5006

E-mail: *asaeldh@hotmail.com*
Web: *www.sweaboston.org*

President: Åsa Eldh

Founded: 1985

Description: To promote Swedish culture and traditions.

Activities: Swedish Yuletide (Christmas Fair), Crayfish party, Shrimp party and a luncheon for recipient of SWEA scholarship.

Publication: Newsletter published three times per year: *SWEA Bladet*

Benefits: Networking and friendship

♛ SWEA, Buffalo

Louise Enhörning
21 Oakland Place
Buffalo, NY 14222

Phone: 716.882.3626

E-mail: *louisee@localnet.com*

♛ SWEA, Chicago

Gunilla Johansson
1950 Chestnut Avenue
Wilmette, IL 60091-1510

E-mail: *chicago@swea.org*
Web: *www.chapters.swea.org/Chicago*

♛ SWEA, Dallas

Tina Klintmalm
3808 Miramar Ave.
Dallas, TX 75205

Phone: 214.526.6468
Fax: 214.522.0148

E-mail: *tinakli@charter.net*
Web: *www.chapters.swea.org/dallas/*

President: Carin Anger

Founded: June 3, 2000

Description: The specific purposes of the organization are to engage in activities related to the support, preservation, promotion and development of Swedish history, culture and traditions in the world; to further worldwide friendship and personal growth among Swedish and Swedish-speaking women; to support education through SWEA International scholarship funds; to assist members of SWEA to adjust and integrate into a new country and when moving back to Sweden; and support projects determined to be of special concern to Swedish women.

Activities: Monthly board meetings, semla celebration, Swedish smörgåsbords, Crayfish dinner, pea soup dinner, Christmas bazaar, St. Lucia and Christmas celebration, garage sales, movie, evenings, museum visits, theaters and plays.

Publication: Quarterly newsletter

♛ SWEA, Denver

Kerstin Karloev
2675 S. Yukon Ct.
Lakewood, CO 80227

Phone: 303.988.3719

E-mail: *denver@swea.org*
Web: *www.swea.org/Denver/index.ht*

SWEA, Hawaii

Lena Galbraith
Kailua, HI

E-mail: *hawaii@swea.org*

 SWEA, Las Vegas

Louise Mishel
Las Vegas, NV

E-mail: *lasvegas@swea.org*

 SWEA, Los Angeles

Berit Hokanson
3663 Keystone Avenue #44
Los Angeles, CA 90034

Phone: 310.204.5182

Web: *www.swea.org*

 SWEA, Michigan

Lill Ingvarson
761 Ten Point Drive
Rochester Hills, MI 48309

E-mail: *michigan@swea.org*
Web: *www.chapter.swea.org/michigan*

♛ SWEA, Minnesota

Britt-Marie Wood
2815 Urbandale Lane North
Plymouth, MN 554417

Phone: 763.475.9112

E-mail: *minnesota@swea.org*
Web: *www.swea.org*

♛ SWEA, New Jersey

Kerstin Casserstedt
5 Kastrel Ln.
Bedminster, NJ 07921

E-mail: *newjersey@swea.org*
Web: *www.chapters.swea.org/NewJersey*

♛ SWEA, New Orleans

Eva Lamothe Trivigno
1831 Marengo Street
New Orleans, LA 70115

Phone: 604.891.1263
E-mail: *evatrivigno@aol.com*

SWEA, New York

Aja Öhman
7 Ronald Ln.
Cos Cob, CT 06807

E-mail: *newyork@swea.org*
Web: *www.chapters.swea.org/newyork*

SWEA, North Carolina

Anette Nordvall
2408 Clerestory Place
Raleigh, NC 27615

Phone: 919.876.1029

E-mail: *northcarolina@swea.org*
Web: *www.swea.org*

SWEA, Orange County

Laila Soares
Orange County, CA

E-mail: *orangecounty@swea.org*

SWEA, Philadelphia

Christina Malmström
Tredyffrin, PA

E-mail: *philadelphia@swea.org*

♛ SWEA, San Diego

Gunnel Schoenherr
11423 Lucera Pl.
San Diego, CA 92127

Phone: 858.485.8706
Fax: 858.485.1935

E-mail: *sandiego@swea.org*
Web: *www.swea.org*

President: Britta Armstrong

Founded: 1981

Description: Keep our Swedish language, support Swedish women, culture, traditions and spread knowledge about Sweden among people in our adopted countries.

Activities: Meetings once a month and a Christmas Fair.

Publication: Local newsletter: *SWEA Bladet*

Benefits: Give scholarships and support to cultural events.

♛ SWEA, San Francisco

Margareta Tönisson
45 Prado Court
Portola Valley, CA 94028

Phone: 650.851.1509
Fax: 650.851.5511

E-mail: *sanfrancisco@swea.org*
Web: *www.chapters.swea.org/SanFran*

SWEA, Santa Barbara

Gun Malmström-Dukes
Carpinteria, CA

E-mail: *santabarbara@swea.org*

♛ SWEA, Seattle

Malin Jonsson
4342 239th Pl. SE
Issaquah, WA 98029

Phone: 425.837.1280

E-mail: *seattle@swea.org*
Web: *www.chapters.swea.org/seattle*

👑 SWEA, South Florida

Britt Norrman
6221 Old Court Road #207
Boca Raton, FL 33433

Phone: 561.395.0959
Fax: 561.395.0959

E-mail: *brittn@earthlink.net*
Web: *www.chapters-swea.org/florida*

President: Britt Norrman

Founded: 1992

Description: To protect and further the Swedish cultural heritage and traditions as well as the Swedish language.

Activities: Networking-evenings every Tuesday of the month, Valborg, Midsummer, Crawfish and Lucia/Christmas Celebrations. For all Swedes, friends, families, whether foreign or Swedish.

Publication: A newsletter published 3 times per year: *SWEA Bladet*

Benefits: To establish personal and professional contacts abroad—all over the world.

♛ SWEA, Texas

Lisa Fugelsang
108 Englewood
Bellaire, TX 77401

Phone: 713.664.1658

E-mail: *cfuglesang@aol.com*

SWEA, Toronto

Ebba Jantz
Toronto, ON

E-mail: *toronto@swea.org*

♛ SWEA, Vancouver

Gun-Britt Fransson
5024 Pinetree Crescent
West Vancouver, BC
V7W 3A3

Phone: 604.926.5246

E-mail: *vancouver@swea.org*

♛ SWEA, Virginia Beach

Anna Maria Asberg
808 Navigator Court
Virginia Beach, VA 23454

Phone: 757.412.1086

E-mail: *virginiabeach@swea.org*

♛ SWEA, Washington DC

Berit Boegli
9013 Fort Craig Drive
Burke, VA 22015

Phone: 703.323.0645
Fax: 703.425.8994

E-mail: *beritb@cox.net*
Web: *www.chapters-swea.org/washingtondc/*

VASA ORDER OF AMERICA

 Vasa Order of America–Grand Lodge

Cynthia Erickson
50 S.E. Bush St.
Issaquah, WA 98027

Phone: 425.392.5420

E-mail: *webmaster@vasaorder.com*
Web: *www.vasaorder.com*

Grand Master: Ulf Brynjestad

Founded: 1896

Description: The Vasa Order of America began more than a
century ago as a benefit fraternal society for Swedish immigrants to the United States. Membership at the time was limited to Swedish-born men who through the Vasa Order met
others who needed to learn the new language and ways of
the new country. A benefit fund provided a small income to
members during sickness, and a death benefit at the time
would cover final expenses. The Order is named for Gustav
Vasa, who liberated the country in the 16th century and
became the first King of modern Sweden. The name of Vasa
reflects the Order's roots as a Swedish American Fraternal
Organization.

Over the past nine decades, many things have changed,
and the Vasa Order has grown to meet the new needs of the
Scandinavian-American community. Whereas in the past
members looked to Vasa to help them learn the ways of the

new country and provide them a means to share problems and solutions with their countrymen, today Vasa provides members a means to share their rich heritage with fellow Americans, and helps them to learn or remember the meaningful ways and values of the "Old Country."

Swedish in origin, the Vasa Order welcomes men and women over 14 years of age of Scandinavian roots (Swedish, Norwegian, Danish, Finnish or Icelandic) and their spouses, who would like to rediscover the traditions of their forefathers or share their Scandinavian heritage. We do this by encouraging the observance of special dates, old and new, such as Midsummer, Leif Ericksson Day, etc. with proper festivities including Smorgasbord and Scandinavian music. While much of our activity occurs during the summer season, in mid-December it is hard to find a Vasa Lodge where Luciafest is not observed.

There are nearly three hundred lodges in the Vasa Order, governed by 19 District Lodges in the United States, Sweden and Canada. The most popular monthly meeting nights are Friday and Wednesday. While you may apply for membership to any of our lodges, if you were to join the closest one to your home you would find it easier to participate in meetings and activities.

Activities: Many lodges or districts sponsor language classes as well as children's clubs in which folk dances are learned and performed in authentic costume. Whenever we can, we take part in programs where our rich heritage may be shared with the public.

Publications: *VASA Star* (America), *VASA Nytt* (Sweden)— both membership news bulletins.

VOA–Anchor Lodge #648

Garden Grove, CA

VOA–Arlington Lodge #62

Hackettstown, NJ

VOA–Astor Lodge #215

Astoria, OR

VOA–Austin Lodge #466

Chicago, IL

VOA–Balder Lodge #308

Washington, PA

VOA–Balder Lodge #343

Eureka, CA

VOA–Baltic Lodge #689

Green Valley Lake, CA

VOA–Baltic-Framåt Lodge #360

New Milford, NJ

VOA–Bessemer Lodge #203

Palos Park, IL

👑 VOA–Birka Lodge #732

Linnea Christianson
105 Pearl Street
Woburn, MA 01801

Phone: 781.933.4949

Web: *www.vasaorder.com*

👑 VOA–Bishop Hill Lodge #683

Roger Anderson
P.O. Box 5
Bishop Hill, IL 61419-0117

Phone: 309.932.3403

E-mail: *rj3640@bwsys.net*
Web: *www.vasaorder.com*

Chairman: Roger W. Anderson

Founded: 1968

Description: A not-for-profit organization, consisting of Scandinavians, Scandinavian-Americans, their spouses and children. Provide a focal point for celebrating our shared cultural ethnicity. Nordic heritage is shared through educational programs, Swedish language lessons, holiday celebrations and the Vasa Archives.

Activities: Pea soup and pancake supper, district convention, Midsommar celebration, Lucia smörgåsbord and program in December.

Publication: A newsletter, 3 times per year.

Benefits: Provide assistance to members in time of illness or death (old age and benefit pay, hospital benefits, funeral fund), college scholarships and student loans are available. Swedish language lessons and heritage educational programs each month by a cultural leader.

VOA–Brage-Iduna Lodge #9

Longmeadow, MA

VOA–Brahe Lodge #245

Geneva, IL

VOA–Branting Lodge #417

Calgary, AB

VOA–Branting Lodge #477

Kris Gealy
PO Box 2304
Laramie, WY 82073

VOA–Cariboo Lodge #690

Quesnel, BC

♕ VOA–Carl Larsson Lodge #739

James Gulick
11008 Mason Ridge Dr.
Raleigh, NC 27614

Phone: 919.676.8607

E-mail: *rgulick@nc.rr.com*
Web: *www.vasaorder.com*

Chairman: Paul Hollinghurst

♔ VOA–Carl Widen Lodge #743

Alice Stried
P.O. Box 4204
Austin, TX 78765

Phone: 512.759.6011

Web: *www.vasaorder.com*

♔ VOA–Carl XVI Gustav Lodge #716

Alan Strom
P.O. Box 830592
Richardson, TX 75082

Phone: 972.690.4331

E-mail: *alan.p.strom@prodigy.net*
Web: *www.geocities.com/~kcole/c16gvasa.htm*

VOA–Dalahäst Lodge #742

Lincroft, NJ

♛ VOA–Desert Viking Lodge #682

Ila Engstrom
38-100 Vicki Lane
Cathedral City, CA 92234

Phone: 760.328.1754

VOA–Diana Birger Jarl #3

Old Saybrook, CT

♛ VOA–District Lodge Alberta No. 18

Thelma Spielman
6116 Dalbeattie Hill NW
Calgary, AB
T3A 1MB

Phone: 403.288.6948

E-mail: *tmspielman@shaw.ca*

VOA–Draken Lodge #731

Stanhope, NJ

♛ VOA–Drott Lodge #168

Ronald Carlson
616 Putnam Pl.
Alexandria, VA 22303

Phone: 703.549.5908

E-mail: *rcarl616@msn.com*
Web: *www.geocities.com/drottlodge*

♛ VOA–Enighet Lodge #178

Roland Nilsson
13558 W. Alaska Dr.
Lakewood, CO 80228

Phone: 303.985.3538

E-mail: *Ekenskis@aol.com*
Web: *www.vasaorder.com*

♛ VOA–Eskilstuna Lodge #633

Hans-Olof Söderström
Eneby 1156 A
SE-635 09 Eskilstuna
Sweden

E-mail: *hans-olof.s@telia.com*

VOA–Evening Star Lodge #426

Hawaiian Gardens, CA

VOA–Excelsior Lodge #435

Renton, WA

VOA–Facklan Lodge #248

Ellen Urie
2136 S. 48th Terrace
Kansas City, KS 66106

Phone: 913.677.0088

♛ VOA–FokusLodge #681

Joan Carlson Walson
1473 Atlanta Court
Florence, KY 41042

Phone: 859.384.3615

E-mail: *jcwalson@juno.com*

Secretary: Joan Carlson Walson
Founded: 1967

Description: Fraternal Organization. Cultural and social activities. Celebrate Swedish Heritage

Activities: Monthly meetings with picnics or potlucks at members' homes or meetings at restaurants, Valborgsmässoafton, Midsommar,Lucia celebration and a "Crayfish" picnic.

Publication: Newsletter

Benefits: Cultural/Social

VOA–Forsgard-Olson Lodge #757

Waco, TX

VOA–Fram Lodge #267

Farmington, MI

VOA–Framåt Lodge #166

Sandstone, MN

 VOA–Framåt Lodge #405

Joan Graham
5838 San Jose Avenue
Richmond, CA 94804

Phone: 510.526.5512

E-mail: *vasajlg@aol.com*

VOA–Framåt Lodge #463

Escanaba, MI

☙ VOA–Freja Lodge #100

Don S. Jacobson
P.O. Box 43
Pleasantville, NY 10570

☙ VOA–Frihet Lodge #401

Karla Anderson
715 N. 79th Street
Seattle, WA 98103-4711

E-mail: *karlaa@nwlink.com*

VOA–Frihiof Lodge #63

Parsippany, NJ

♚ VOA–Fylgia Lodge #119

Richard L. Wooster II
3400 Anza Street #2
San Francisco, CA 94121

♚ VOA–Glenn T. Seaborg Lodge #719

Lily Nelson
524 Calle Aragon Unit Q
Laguna Woods, CA 92653

Phone: 949.837.9926

Web: *www.vasaorder.com*

VOA–Gold Nugget Lodge #662

Magalia, CA

VOA–Golden Valley Lodge #616

Sherman Oaks, CA

♛ VOA–Göta Lejon Lodge #251

Linda Schueler
2703 Highway 3
Two Harbors, MN 55616

Phone: 218.834.2624

Chairman: Linda Schueler

Founded: 1923

Activities: St. Lucia festival and participation in Heritage Days with a Lutefisk Challenge and Parade Float

Benefits: *Nordic Reach* magazine, fellowship and cultural exploration

VOA–Göta Lejon Lodge #84

Yorktown Heights, NY

VOA–Göta Lejon-Ingeborg Lodge #19

Southington, CT

VOA–Gothiod Lodge #486

Kenvil, NJ

VOA–Gustav V Lodge #175

Lemon Grove, CA

VOA–Hagar Lodge #721

Des Plaines, IL

♛ VOA–Harmoni Lodge #472

Patricia McLean
3801 S.E. Crystal Springs Blvd.
Portland, OR 97202

Phone: 503.775.9932

E-mail: *sundvall@hevanet.com*
Web: *www.hevanet.com/sundvall/vasa*

VOA–Harmony Lodge #465

Struthers, OH

VOA–Hemmet Lodge #748

Hemet, CA

VOA–Höga Nord Lodge #194

Lyndhurst, NJ

VOA–Holiday Lodge #699

Gulfport, FL

VOA–Ingeborg Lodge #66

E. Bridgewater, MA

♛ VOA–Ishpeming Lodge #196

Marilyn Andrew
624 Elliot Avenue
Ishpeming, MI 49849

Phone: 906.485.5140

E-mail: *marilandre@aol.com*

Chair: Barbara Nuorala

Founded: July 29, 1911

Description: Learn about Scandinavian heritage, culture and fellowship.

Benefits: Summer picnic and a Christmas party

VOA–Jenny Lind Lodge #388

Turlock, CA

VOA–Joe Harbor Lodge #534

Benton Harbor, MI

VOA–Johan Banér #36

Warwick, RI

VOA–John Ericsson Lodge #25

Marlene Patient
21 Richards Street
Worcester, MA 01603

Phone: 508.791.7241

Web: *www.vasaorder.com*

VOA–John Morton Lodge #488

542 E. Idaho Ave.
St. Paul, MN 55101

Phone: 651.771.6780

♛ VOA–Jubilee Lodge #692

Randrea Derstine
127 Lake Charles Road
DeLand, FL 32724

Phone: 386.736.7443

E-mail: *randycleon@hotmail.com*

♛ VOA–Jubileum Lodge #755

Barbara Mittelstaedt
816 Butternut Road
Madison, WI 53704

Phone: 608.249.2912
Fax: 608.249.2912

E-mail: *barbaram_53704@yahoo.com*
Web: *www.vasaweb.com*

Chair: Lowell Nordling

Founded: November 17, 1996

Description: The main objective of Jubileum Lodge is to celebrate our common Scandinavian heritage.

Activities: The organization meets monthly from September
through June. The monthly meetings typically include lectures on subjects of interest to the members. We also have

our annual Julfest (with a smörgåsbord and Sancta Lucia program) and a Midsummer celebration.

Publication: *Vasa Views*

Benefits: Jubileum Lodge offers its members good fellowship and the opportunity to learn more about Scandinavian history and culture.

VOA–Karl XII #103

Plainville, CT

VOA–Klippan Lodge #228

Seattle, WA

♛ VOA–Kronan Lodge #179

Virginia Lindroos
4200 N. Francisco
Chicago, IL 60618

Phone: 773.463.8477

♔ VOA–Kronan Lodge #2

Britt Nordlund
140 Old Mill Road
Wilton, CT 06897

VOA–Kronan Lodge #433

Woodbury, MN

VOA–Lethbridge Lodge #579

Lethbridge, AB

♔ VOA–Lindbergh Lodge #494

Gun Wastholm-McCuen
27010 Dezahara Way
Los Altos Hills, CA 94022

♔ VOA–Lindbergh Lodge #505

Sven Steen
1661 Old Country Rd. Lot 295
Riverhead, NY 11901-4412

Phone: 631.727.7045

VOA–Linde Lodge #492

Lisa Ekstrand, Secretary
15070 Mayflower Dr.
New Berlin, WI 53151

Phone: 262.782.2238

E-mail: *lekstrand@wi.rr.com*

Chair: Margaret Gruel

Founded: June, 1927

Description: We are a fraternal organization. We promote genuine understanding of our culture through songs, printed articles, and visiting the infirm.

Activities: Scandinavian Fest, Picnic and a Pea Soup and Pancake Supper.

Publication: Monthly newsletter to all members, friends of Vasa and interested clubs throughout the USA and Sweden.

Benefits: Helping hands for those that need it. Old age benefits for the infirm.

VOA–Lindgren Lodge #754

Joanne Schroeder
3168 West Point Road
Green Bay, WI 54313

Phone: 920.494.1728

E-mail: *howiewho@aol.com*
Web: *www.ez.net/~roblnls/vasa.htm*

Chair: Janice Nelson

Founded: October 10, 1995

Description: Interested in preserving the culture of our lands
and in maintaining close ethnic contact with our fellow
Scandinavians.

Activities: Pea soup and Pancake dinner, Midsommer, fish boil
and St. Lucia

Publication: Newsletter: *Vasa Posten*

VOA–Lindholmen Lodge #670

Medicine Hat, AB

 VOA–Linné Lodge #153

Agnes Swanson
4544 Crawford Court
South Bend, IN 46614

Phone: 574.299.0454

VOA–Linné Lodge #429

Summit, NJ

VOA–Linnea Lodge #174

Silver Bow, MT

👑 VOA–Linnea Lodge #504

Linnea Koagedal
14 Steven Drive
Petaluma, CA 94952

Phone: 707.763.1080

E-mail: *linneak@pacbell.net*

VOA–Linnea Lodge #696

Escondido, CA

VOA–Lyckan Lodge #507

Somerset, NJ

VOA–Manhem Lodge #159

Menominee, MI

VOA–Mayflower Lodge #445

Palos Verdes, CA

👑 VOA–Miami Lodge #554

Jean Dahlgren
2100 Laurel Lane
N. Miami, FL 33181

Phone: 305.891.2606

E-mail: *FJDCI@yahoo.com*

👑 VOA–Minnesota District Lodge #7

Janice Lehman
3109 32nd Avenue S.
Minneapolis, MN 55406

Web: *www.vasaorder.com*

VOA–Monitor Lodge #163

Ishpeming, MI

VOA–Monitor Lodge #218

Sacramento, CA

VOA–Mount Vernon Lodge #485

Malden, MA

VOA–Nobel Lodge #184

Elsie Nordby
11869 S.E. 33rd
Milwaukie, OR 9722-6811

Phone: 503.654.6629

E-mail: *lisaellsberg@att.net*
Web: *www.vasaorder.com*

VOA–Nobel Lodge #288

Bettendorf, IA

VOA–Nobel-Liljan Lodge #64

W. Hempstead, NY

♛ VOA–Nobel-Monitor Lodge #130

Mrs. Marty Bergman
3236 Berkeley Avenue
Cleveland Heights, OH 44118-2055

Phone: 216.371.5141
Fax: 216.274.9664

E-mail: *martyb@apk.net*

Chair: Mrs. Marty Bergman

Founded: January 1908

Description: To perpetuate the Nobel heritage of our forefathers and to foster Scandinavian cultural activities, traditions, and customs. To pass this history and culture on to the younger and coming generations.

Activities: Midsummer celebration, Lucia with Vasa Voices, Pea soup and Plättar meal, Korv meal, spring concert with Vasa Voices singing in Swedish, and the weekly meetings of the "Breakfast Club."

Publication: Monthly newsletter

Benefits: Members of five years may apply for financial help— up to a total of $2000.00 in a lifetime. $20,000.00 in college scholarships each year, ten scholarships for youth 12-18 for language camp. Also a student loan program ($1,500 annual maximum with $4,500 total loan amount).

VOA–Nord Lodge #392

Ione, CA

VOA–Norden Lodge #513

Bashaw, AB

VOA–Norden Lodge #1

Wethersfield, CT

♛ VOA–Norden Lodge #233

Shirlyanne Sargent
P.O. Box 64008
Tacoma, WA 98464

Phone: 253.565.2346

VOA–Norden Lodge #310

St. Paul, MN

VOA–Norden Lodge #684

Fresno, CA

VOA–Nordic Heritage Lodge #741

Valencia, CA

♛ VOA–Nordic Lodge #611

Siw Kristiansson
39 Mountainshire Drive
Worcester, MA 01606

Phone: 508.852.8082

E-mail: *siw-leif@msn.com*
Web: *www.vasaorder.com*

♛ VOA–Nordic Lodge #660

Arlene Lundquist
14761 Crosswood Rd.
La Mirada, CA 90638

Phone: 714.521.3791
Fax: 714.521.3791

E-mail: *alund18@earthlink.net*

Chair: LeRoy Anderson

Founded: 1961

Description: Open to Scandinavian persons interested in keeping in touch with their roots and culture.

Activities: Pancake Breakfast, Lutfisk Dinner, Lucia and Midsommar.

Publication: Newsletter: 6 times per year

Benefits: Scholarship opportunities, genealogy research and speaking Swedish.

 VOA–Nordic Lodge #708

Laurie Fulton
5317 Slater Mill Circle
Douglasville, GA 30135-1203

Phone: 770.949.6667

E-mail: *lfulton@co.douglas.ga.us*

Activities: Monthly meeting/event August-June celebrating holidays, traditions, culture, foods and history of Scandinavia. Frequent outdoor activities-hiking, rafting and picnicing.

Publication: Perodic newsletter and frequent e-mail

VOA–Nordstjärnan #575

Wetaskiwin, AB

VOA–Nornan Lodge #413

Mission, BC

VOA–Norrskenet Lodge #189

Ocean Park, WA

♛ VOA–Norrskenet Lodge #331

Harland Johnson
4655 Ravine Park Dr.
Sioux City, IA 51106-4404

Phone: 712.276.7468

Chair: Harland Johnson

Founded: October 27, 1915

Description: The main goal of the Vasa Norrskenet Lodge #331 is to preserve Scandinavian culture and to support youth and education.

Activities: Monthly meetings (except June, July and August), Christmas Swedish Smorgasbord, Swedish yellow pea soup and Swedish pancake luncheon.

Benefits: Cultural programs, ethnic festivals, and Scandinavian fellowship.

VOA–North Star Lodge #106

Glendale, CA

👑 VOA–North Star Lodge #145

Marilyn Tomson
6804 N. Fleming
Spokane, WA 99208

Phone: 509.328.4085

Web: *www.geocities.com/Heartland/Prairie/9644*

VOA–Northern Light Lodge #620

Oxnard, CA

VOA–Northlanders Lodge #723

Scottsdale, AZ

VOA–Oak Leaf Lodge #685

Thousand Oaks, CA

♛ VOA–Odin Lodge #726

Richard G. Maris, Cultural Leader
513 Pinto Way
Eugene, OR 97401

Phone: 541.345.4566
Fax: 541.344.3332

E-mail: *rgmaris@msn.com*

President: Kathy Saranpa

Founded: December, 1979

Description: Vasa enables members to learn the traditions of their forefathers and share their rich heritage with other Americans.

Activities: Monthly meetings, Midsummer, St. Lucia celebration and Swedish language classes.

Publication: Monthly newsletter

VOA–Olympia Lodge #550

Shelton, WA

♛ VOA–Olympic Lodge #235

Lois Erickson
6 Apache Way
Branchburg, NJ 08876

E-mail: *lcerickson@att.net*

VOA–Omaha Lodge #330

Omaha, NE

VOA–Örn Lodge #284

Old Tappan, NJ

♛ VOA–Oscars Borg Lodge #172

Linda J. Smith
3125 Mill Road
Doylestown, PA 18901

Phone: 215.794.5950
Fax: 215.794.5950

E-mail: *dale.o.smith@verizon.net*

Chair: Lori Ackerman

Instituted: March 2, 1910

Activities: Monthly meetings (the fourth Sunday), excluding July and August, at Bethesda Presbyterian Church.

Publication: Monthly newsletter

Benefits: Financial aid and scholarships.

👑 VOA–Phoenix Lodge #677

Art & Elna Lidman
2331 North 66th Street
Scottsdale, AZ 85257

Phone: 480.946.8763

VOA–Pioneer Lodge #506

Cranston, RI

VOA–Quahog Lodge #725

Wakefield, RI

VOA–Quinsigamond Lodge #517

W. Boylston, MA

♔ VOA–Red Deer Lodge #733

Frida Johnson
23 Ellenwood Drive
Red Deer, AB
T4R 2E1

Phone: 403.342.7864

VOA–Redligheten Lodge #493

Youngwood, PA

VOA–Reno Lodge #711

Reno, NV

VOA–Royal Palm Lodge #645

Maj-Britt Wesley
2803 S.W. 14th Court
Deerfield Beach, FL 33442

Phone: 954.427.9987
Fax: 954.427.6907

VOA–Runan Magnet Lodge #120

Buffalo, NY

VOA–Runeberg Lodge #137

Franklin Dietrich
3800 10th Ave. S.
Minneapolis, MN 55407

Phone: 612.822.0039

♛ VOA–Satellite Lodge #661

Portage, MI

VOA–Scandia Lodge #728

Prescott Valley, AZ

VOA–Scandia Lodge#23

Manchester, CT

VOA–Scandinavian Lodge #667

La Mesa, CA

VOA–Sierra Kronan Lodge #737

Loomis, CA

VOA–Siljan-Mora-Tuna Lodge #134

Midlothian, IL

VOA–Skandia Lodge #247

Pasadena, CA

VOA–Skandia Lodge #356

Watchung, NJ

VOA–Skandia Lodge #399

New York City, NY

VOA–Skandia Lodge #549

Edmonton, AB

VOA–Skogen Lodge #700

Redding, CA

VOA–Skogsblomman Lodge #378

Bothell, WA

👑 VOA–Småland Lodge #618

Rune Fornander
Resedastigen 9
SE-554 56 Jönköping
Sweden

VOA–Solidaritet Lodge #396

Anacortes, WA

VOA–Solstad Lodge #709

Sun City West, AZ

VOA–Spiran Lodge #98

Rockport, MA

VOA–Star Lodge #56

Coventry, RI

VOA–Stenbock Lodge #138

Ronald Swanson
2222 E. Old Shakopee Rd.
Bloomington, MN 55425

Phone: 952.854.8192

 VOA–Stenland Lodge #727

Inger Terzakis
29 Greenridge Way
Spring Valley, NY 10977

Phone: 845.354.6025

VOA–Strindberg Lodge #259

Winnipeg, MB

VOA–Superior Lodge #423

Marquette, MI

 VOA–Svea Lodge #253

Janet Jegen, Recording Secretary
8690 Jaffa Ct. W. Dr.
Indianapolis, IN 46260

Phone: 317.844.9924

E-mail: *nubangmd@cs.com*
Web: *www.vasaorder.com*

VOA–Svea Lodge #296

Erie, PA

VOA–Svea Lodge #340

Staten Island, NY

VOA–Svea Lodge #348

Toni Bray, Secretary
140 Cherokee Way
Portola Valley, CA 94028

Phone: 650.851.8177

E-mail: *secretary@svea348.org*
Web: *www.svea348.org*

Chair: Axel Jonasson

Founded: August 20, 1916

Description: A Scandinavian-American fraternal organization, Svea Lodge #348 is a fellowship that shares a common interest in Scandinavian culture and heritage.

Activities: Valborgsmässoafton celebration, Midsummer in Sveadal, Fourth of July pancake breakfast, Lucia, Smorgasbord.

Publication: Monthly newsletter: *Svea Bladet*

VOA–Svea Lodge #362

Providence, RI

VOA–Svea Lodge #469

Longview, WA

VOA–Sveaborg Lodge #446

Hackettstown, NJ

♛ VOA–Sveaborg Lodge #449

Evelyn Ternstrom
1377 Milton Ave.
Walnut Creek, CA 94596

Phone: 925.279.4301

E-mail: *ternstrm@ix.netcom.com*
Web: *www.vasaorder.com*

Chair: Ray Ternstrom

Founded: June 1924

Description: The organization provides the opportunity to
share in fellowship with men and women of Scandinavian
heritage while celebrating holiday and cultural events.
     Main goal: to preserve and promote the Scandinavian cul-
tural heritage.

Activities: Pea soup and oven pancake dinner (ärtsoppa och
ugnspannkaka), Swedish pancake breakfast fundraiser, crayfish and meatballs (kräftskiva och köttbullar), Christmas
party (julfest med smörgåsbord), Lucia celebration,
Midsommar at Sveadal and participation in Sweden Day.

Publication: Newsletter: *Sveaborg Lodge Newsletter*

Benefits: Scandinavian friendships, cultural events, scholarships, Swedish language classes, and publications of
Scandinavian interest.

VOA–Tegnér Lodge #109

Glenville, NY

 ## VOA–Tegnér Lodge #149

Elsy Mattson
9042 Craydon Circle
San Ramon, CA 94583

Phone: 925.833.1749

E-mail: *elsym@pacbell.net*

VOA–Tegnér Lodge #224

Alice Comstock
1824 River Road
Missoula, MT 59801

Phone: 406.542.0253

President: Bruce Swanson

Founded: early 1900s

Description: Tegnér Lodge #224 is a fraternal organization whose main purpose is to sponsor and promote Swedish culture and heritage within the community.

Activities: Annual scholarship given to a graduating senior, participation in the University of Montana's International Food Festival, and hosting an annual Swedish Bazaar in November.

VOA–Tegnér-Valkyrian Lodge #5

Marlborough, CT

VOA–Thor Lodge #147

Channahon, IL

VOA–Three Crown Lodge #91

Lynn, MA

VOA–Three Crown Lodge #38

Norwalk, CT

VOA–Three Crowns Lodge #704

Pompton Plains, NJ

♛ VOA–Thule Lodge #127

Lucille Marsh
6670 Charlotte Center Road
Sinclairville, NY 14782-9612

♛ VOA–Thule Lodge #467

Jane Sandler
225 North Irving Blvd.
Los Angeles, CA 90004

Phone: 323.463.5394

VOA–Thule Lodge #96

Beverly, MA

♛ VOA–Thule Lodge Swedish Folk Dancers No. 19

Donna Johnson
806 Forest Drive
Jamestown, NY 14701

Phone: 716.483.3829

E-mail: *dnjbaj@madbbs.com*

♛ VOA–Travelers Vasa #758

Marjorie Matetzschk
1227 Lake Terrace Dr.
Elgin, TX 78621

Phone: 512.281.3860

E-mail: *matetzschk100@msn.com*

Activities: Meets 4th Saturday, 11 a.m., at the Yegua Creek
    Evangelical Free Church, 1200 CR 466, Elgin, TX 78621.

♛ VOA–Tre Kronor Lodge #713

Roger Danielson
688 Danielson Lane
Stayton, OR 97383-2238

Phone: 503.769.5138

E-mail: *rogerd@wvi.com*
Web: *http://home.teleport.com/~ostrom*

VOA–Trofast Lodge #231

Everett, WA

VOA–Trygg Lodge #536

North Muskegon, MI

♛ VOA–Tryggve Lodge #88

Carl Erickson
109 S. Prospect Street
Verona, NJ 07044

Web: *www.vasaorder.com*

VOA–Tucson Lodge #691

Tucson, AZ

VOA–Vågen Lodge #588

Brick, NJ

♛ VOA–Valhalla Lodge #715

Ann McKenna
621 Callahan Point Drive
Las Vegas, NV 89145

Phone: 702.869.5037

Web: *www.vasaorder.com*

♛ VOA–Valhalla Scandinavians Lodge #746

Chuck and Barbara Olson
P.O. Box 2411
Santa Cruz, CA 95063

Phone: 831.438.4307
Fax: 831.438.4307

E-mail: *chuck@olsonconnection.com*
Web: *www.scandinavians-santacruz.org*

Founder: Robert H. Peterson

Founded: October 1, 1989

Description: Our main goal it to perpetuate the noble heritage
of our forefathers and to foster Scandinavian cultural activities by encouragement and example to our members.

Activities: Monthly presentation of Scandinavian culture,
Midsummer celebration, Lucia with 40–50 children, pea
soup and pancakes in March, semlor during Lent and
monthly planning meetings.

Publication: Monthly newsletter: *Voice of Valhalla*

Benefits: Members of Valhalla receive discounted prices for dinners, etc; participation in Vasa activities on the district level
and international.

VOA–Valley Vikings Lodge #701

Bakersfield, CA

VOA–Vasa Hope Lodge #503

Seattle, WA

♛ VOA–Viking Lodge #256

Steven Leigard
21402 S. Perry Street
Carson, CA 90745

♛ VOA–Viking Lodge #730

Eric Swanson
8433 McKinley Road
Flushing, MI 48433

Phone: 310.733.5025

E-mail: *ceswan@centurytel.net*
Web: *www.vasaorder.com*

VOA–Viking Lodge #735

Bethlehem, PA

VOA–Viking Lodge #756

Greenfield, MA

VOA–Viking Lodge #621

Pomfret Center, CT

VOA–Viljan Lodge #349

Sycamore, IL

VOA–Vinland of Cape Cod Lodge #703

South Harwich, MA

VOA–Williamson County Lodge #753

Taylor, TX

Organizations in Canada

The organizations and institutions in this section include Swedish-Canadian and Scandinavian-Canadian groups, as well as other organizations—such as museums, churches, non-profit organizations, and social clubs—that promote the culture and heritage of Sweden and/or Scandinavia in Canada.

 indicates the organization is an affiliate of the Swedish Council of America

Canadian Nordic Society

Per Olav Talgøy
P.O. Box 55023
240 Sparks St.
Ottawa, ON
K1P 1A1

Phone: 613.260.9066
Fax: 613.991.1879

E-mail: *admin@canadiannordicsociety.com*
Web: *www.canadiannordicsociety.com*

President: Per Olav Talgøy

Founded: September, 1963

Description: Based in Canada's National Capital Region, the
Canadian Nordic Society celebrates the links and common
interests between Canada and the Nordic countries: Iceland,
Norway, Denmark, Sweden and Finland. For 40 years the
CNS has provided opportunities to share, learn, and celebrate Nordic culture and history and Canada's Nordic connection.

Activities: The Canadian Nordic Society hosts a program of
speakers, organizes events and celebrations.

Publication: Newsletter, *Nordic News*

Benefits: Members receive the Society's newsletter with news,
information and schedule of events. Discounted admission
to CNS events.

♛ Lakehead Social History Institute

Dr. A. Ernst Epp
History Department, Lakehead University
955 Oliver Road
Thunder Bay, ON
P7B 5E1

Phone: 807.767.0934
Fax: 807.767.0934

E-mail: *barr@swedesincanada.ca*
Web: *www.swedesincanada.ca*

Co-Director: Dr. A. Ernst Epp

Description: Very little serious research has been undertaken so far about the history of Swedes in Canada. One of the reasons is that, unlike the resources available for documentation of some other ethnic cultural groups, there is no specific funding for the Swedish-Canadian experience. The Lakehead Social History Institute, recognizing this lack, has taken up the challenge to sponsor the Swedes in Canada project.

♛ The Lingonberries

Marianne Lundstrom
3-37 MacDonald Street
Ottawa, ON
K2P 1H3

Phone: 613.237.0013

E-mail: *lingonberries@rogers.com*
Web: *www.thelingonberries.com*

Description: The Lingonberries are a bilingual (English and
    Swedish) three-woman/one man a cappella quartet based in
    Ottawa, Canada. Their repertoire centers around traditional
    Swedish folk songs, although three of the four recently
    moved to Canada from Sweden and audiences are hearing
    more and more English lyrics.

Recordings: 2 CDs, "...Summer" and "...Winter."

♛ Reford Gardens

Alexander Reford
200 Route 132
Grand Metis, Quebec
G0J I2O

Phone: 418.775.8306
Fax: 418.775.6201

E-mail: *reford@refordgardens.com*
Web: *www.refordgardens.com*

Founded: September 1961

Description: The primary objective of the organization is to
    maintain the gardens and buildings and to preserve their

unique character. The organization also has an educational and cultural mission. It is responsible for fundraising activities and campaigns to assist the organization in the realization of its objectives.

Activities: The International Garden Festival is the only festival of its kind in North America. The Festival takes place on the site of Reford Gardens every summer since 2000 from the end of June to mid-September. Musical events, summer school, Literary Teas (in French), and lectures.

Scandinavian Businessmen's Club of British Columbia

Ben Marklund
6540 Thomas Street
Burnaby, BC
V5V 4P9

Phone: 604.524.2915

E-mail: *business@scandinaviancentre.org*
Web: *www.scandinaviancentre.org/sbmc*

President: Henrik Laursen

Founded: 1946

Description: The Scandinavian Businessmen's Club of BC is a social club of networking for businesspeople.

Activities: Meets on the 2nd Wednesday of each month. Meetings include a guest speaker with Scandinavian food

and drink. Participation in Midsummer Fest at the
Scandinavian Centre. One or two scholarships given yearly
to children (post secondary) who are related to a current
member.

Scandinavian Canadian Club of Metropolitan Toronto

91 Stormont Avenue
Toronto, ON
M5N 2C3

Phone: 416.782.4604

President: Grethe Papagiorgia

Scandinavian Centre

6540 Thomas Street
Burnaby, BC
V5B 4P9

Phone: 604.294.2777

Scandinavian Club of Regina

P.O. Box 22211
Regina, SK
S4S 7H4

Scandinavian Cultural Centre

764 Erin Street
Winnipeg, MB
R3G 2W4

Phone: 204.774.8047

♛ Scandinavian Home Society

Barbara Ricciardi, Recording Secretary
147 Algoma St. S.
Thunder Bay, ON
P7B 3B7

Phone: 807.345.7742

E-mail: *scandi@vianet.ca*
Web: *www.scandirestaurant.com*

President: Don St. Denis
Founded: November 1923

Description: The purpose of the Scandinavian Home Society is to act as a centre for those who support, appreciate and wish to preserve and promote Scandinavian culture.

Activities: A Fall Tea is held as well as pancake breakfasts the last Sunday of the month as a fund raiser. Functions for specific events are held at Christmas and Mid-summer.

Publication: *The Scandinavian Home Society 1923–1993 — A place to Meet, A Place to Eat, a history of the Society,* by Elinor Barr.

Scandinavian Society of Nova Scotia

31 Ilsley Avenue
Dartmouth, NS
B3B 1L5

Svenska Klubben i Montreal

E-mail: *pernilla@sprint.ca*
Web: *www.svenskaklubben.just.nu*

Director: Pernilla Pålsson

SWEA, Toronto

Toronto, ON

E-mail: *toronto@swea.org*

Director: Ebba Jantz

 SWEA, Vancouver

Gun-Britt Fransson
5024 Pinetree Crescent
West Vancouver, BC
V7W 3A3

Phone: 604.926.5246

E-mail: *vancouver@swea.org*

Swedish Canadian Chamber of Commerce/ Canadian Swedish Business Association

Monika G. Lindmark, Executive Director
2 Bloor Street West, Suite 504
Toronto, ON
M4W 3E2

Phone: 416.929.8661
Fax: 416.929.8639

E-mail: *mail@sccc.ca*
Web: *www.sccc.ca*

Chair: Lars Henriksson

History:
   SCCC Founded: 1965, **CSBA Founded:** 1994
   Merged: January 1, 2002

Description: SCCC-CSBA is a business organization with
   offices in Toronto, Halifax, Montreal and Stockholm that
   focuses on trade, commercial, cultural and social contacts
   between Sweden and Canada.

Activities: SCCC-CSBA organizes business events, such as seminars and conferences, breakfast and lunch meetings with
   keynote speakers, company visits as well as social networking
   opportunities across Canada. Also hosts two annual events
   which draw a large attendance: golf tournament each
   September and a Lucia luncheon each December.

Publication: *SCCCNews*

Benefits: Expands your contact base, assists in promoting products and services, introduces Swedish newcomers to Canada
   and exporters to Sweden, gives you access to a vast array of
   information and resources, and encourages and promotes
   trade and commerce between Canada and Sweden.

Sub Chapters of SCCC/CSBA:

SCCC/CSBA Halifax Chapter

E-mail: *jim.sotvedt@ns.sympatico.ca*

Director: James Sotvedt

SCCC/CSBA Montreal Chapter

E-mail: *polat@technopar.com*

Director: Peter Polatos

Swedish Canadian Club

1800 Duthie Avenue
Burnaby, BC
B5A 2R8

Swedish Cultural Association of Manitoba

Mari Clovechok
764 Erin Street
Winnipeg, MB
R3G 2W4

Phone: 612.872.1452
Fax: 204.772.1019

Founded: 1983

Description: To promote the preservation of the Swedish culture and language in Manitoba; to promote interaction in the Winnipeg area between people of Swedish origin and others who are interested in being associated with what is Sweden; to act as liaison with similar Swedish associations throughout Canada and the United States.

Activities: Monthly meetings; display of an informational booth in the Scandinavian Center's pavilion.

Publication: *The Viking Time*, published five times a year

Swedish Lutheran Church in Toronto

Markku Suokonautio, Priest
25 Old York Mills Road
Toronto, ON
M2P 1B5

Phone: 416.486.0466
Fax: 416.486.0767

E-mail: *kyrkan@better.net*

Chair: Claes Holmquist

Description: The Swedish Lutheran Church in Toronto offers church services every Sunday as well as special occasion worship such as Christmas and Easter.

Activities: The Swedish Church is also a venue for special events such as the Annual Easter Bazaar and select Swedish cultural events.

Publication: Monthly newsletter, *KyrkoNytt*

Swedish Norrskenet Society

Elinor Barr
104 Ray Blvd.
Thunder Bay, ON
P7B 4C4

Phone: 807.344.8355

Swedish Society of Calgary

Carin Pihl
Site 7, P.O. Box 18
R.R.#1
Millarville, AB
T0L 1K0

Phone: 403.931.0370

E-mail: *pihl@ucalgary.ca*

Swedish Trade Office

2 Bloor Street West, Suite 504
Toronto, ON
M4W 3E2

Phone: 416.922.8152
Fax: 416.929.8639

Web: *www.swedishtrade.com/canada*

President: Johan Ögren

VOA–Branting Lodge #417

Calgary, AB

VOA–Cariboo Lodge #690

Quesnel, BC

 VOA–District Lodge Alberta No. 18

Thelma Spielman
6116 Dalbeattie Hill NW
Calgary, AB
T3A 1MB

Phone: 403.288.6948

E-mail: *tmspielman@shaw.ca*

VOA–Lethbridge #579

Lethbridge, AB

VOA–Lindholmen Lodge #670

Medicine Hat, AB

VOA–Norden Lodge #513

Bashaw, AB

VOA–Nordstjärnan Lodge #575

Wetaskiwin, AB

VOA–Nornan Lodge #413

Mission, BC

♛ VOA–Red Deer Lodge #733

Frida Johnson
23 Ellenwood Drive
Red Deer, AB
T4R 2E1

Phone: 403.342.7864

VOA–Skandia Lodge #549

Edmonton, AB

VOA–Strindberg Lodge #259

Winnipeg, MB

Organizations
in Sweden

A number of agencies and organizations in Sweden play an important role in relations with the United States and Canada. These organizations disseminate information, sponsor exchanges of students and scholars, and provide contact between Americans and Canadians living in Sweden. In some instances, an organization or agency includes Swedish-American relations as part of a broader program of contact between Sweden and other countries.

 indicates the organization is an affiliate of the Swedish Council of America

♛ Emigrant Register

Erik Gustavson
Box 331
SE-651 08 Karlstad
Sweden

Phone: 46 54 61 7720
Fax: 46 54 61 7701

E-mail: *research@emigrantregistret.s.se*
Web: *www.emigrantregistret.s.se*

Director: Erik Gustavson

Founded: 1960

Description: Emigrantregistret/Kinship Center in Karlstad, Sweden is the oldest of the Swedish emigration archives. Its activities were started in 1960 and today it is located in the most appropriate accommodations at the Archives Center in Karlstad. Emigrant Registret/Kinship Center has developed into a modern and dynamic archive which is accessible to researchers on all levels.

♛ Föreningen Svenskar i Världen

Kjell K. Jansson
P.O. Box 5501
Näringslivets Hus, Storgatan 19
SE-114 85 Stockholm
Sweden

Phone: 46 8 783 81 81
Fax: 46 8 660 52 64

E-mail: *svenskar.i.varlden@sviv.se*
Web: *www.sviv.se*

Chair: Peter Forssman, **President:** Ambassador Örjan Berner

Founded: 1938

Description: Main goal is to give support to Swedish residents abroad.

Activities: Selecting "Swede of the Year," and hosting seminars.

Publication: Electronic newsletter 4 times per year

Benefits: Insurance, reductions on various items, scholarships and monetary support.

♛ Hostel

Alison Gerber
Lilla Regementsv. 10–Lag. 207
SE-415 27 Göteborg
Sweden

Phone: 46 76 211 6950

E-mail: *alison@hostelprojects.org*
Web: *www.hostelprojects.org*

President: Alison Gerber

Founded: January 29, 2004

Description: Hostel is an organization dedicated to the support
and presentation of new artwork in public and social spaces.
Hostel has been organized as a nonprofit organization (*ideell
förening*) in Sweden and functions with an administrative
base in Sweden and several "satellite" bases in Sweden and
abroad. Each satellite base consists of a local curator or cura-
torial team who work with Hostel to support artists who
wish to travel to their city to research or present new work.
Hostel makes periodic calls for self-initiated projects which
are open to individual artists or collaborative groups; Hostel
also occasionally initiates projects, events, and exhibitions.

 **Musikförlaget Vallmon**

Margaretha Ericksson
Långgatan 24
SE-68630 Sunne
Sweden

E-mail: *m.spangedal@telia.com*

 **Nordiska Museet**

Christina Mattsson
P.O. Box 27820
SE-115 93 Stockholm
Sweden

Phone: 46 8 5198 560 00
Fax: 46 8 519 545 80

E-mail: *nordiska@nordiskamuseet.se*
Web: *www.nordiskamuseet.se*

Founded: 1888

♕ Riksföreningen Sverigekontakt— The Royal Association for Swedish Culture Abroad

Box 53066
SE-400 14 Göteborg
Sweden

Phone: 46 31 18 00 62
Fax: 46 31 20 99 02

E-mail: *info@sverigekontakt.se*
Web: *www.sverigekontakt.se*

Chair: Bo Ralph

Founded: 1908

Description: The Riksföreningen Sverigekontakt is a membership organization, with members all over the world. The main objective is to be a link for Swedes in the world to keep in contact with their language and their culture.

Activities: Meetings, seminars, conferences, courses, travels and much more!

Publication: Quarterly newsletter, *Sverigekontakt*

Benefits: Reduced prices on Swedish books, free delivery anywhere in the world, special travel opportunities, and more.

♔ Sverige-Amerika Stiftelsen (Sweden-America Foundation)

Anna Hamilton
Box 5280
SE-102 46 Stockholm
Sweden

Phone: 46 8 611 46 11/46 8 611 46 44
Fax: 46 8 611 40 04

E-mail: *info@sweamfo.se*
Web: *www.sweamfo.se*

Honorary Chair: Crown Princess Victoria

Founded: 1919

Description: The Sverige-Amerika Stiftelsen was established in June 1919 at the initiative of a group of preeminent scientists, businesses leaders and molders of public opinion. Among the founders and first Board members were Svante Arrhenius, Axel Ax:son Johnson, Jacob Wallenberg, Hjalmar Branting, Selma Lagerlöf, Torgny Segerstedt, The Svedberg, Nathan Söderblom and Anders Zorn.

According to the Foundation's statutes, the objectives are to work for the development of a relationship between Sweden on the one hand, and the United States of America and Canada on the other, by promoting the exchange of scientific, cultural and practical experiences between the countries.

Activities: The range of activities include: presenting fellowships for research and graduate level education in the United States and Canada; arranging scholarships for undergraduate studies in the United States and Canada; arranging visa certificates for students training in the United States; providing information and counseling about higher education in the United States and Canada.

Publication: A newsletter for members, sent out once a year before Christmas, and a book by Dag Blanck, *The First 70 Years of Sverige-Amerika Stiftelsen* (in Swedish)

♛ Swedish American Bicentennial Fellowship Fund

Anders H. Pers
Box 7434
SE-103 91 Stockholm
Sweden

Phone: 46 220 17565

E-mail: *ahp@vlt.se*

Chairman: Amb. Håkan Berggren

Founded: 1976

Description: The Bicentennial Fund, a Swedish tribute to the U.S. Bicentennial, financed by contributions from Sweden's public and private sectors, offers travel grants to American and Swedish professionals who are in a position to influence public opinion.

Benefits: Annual fellowships covering expenses for one month study visits to Sweden and America respectively

♔ Swedish Emigrant Institute/House of Emigrants

Per Nordahl, Director
P.O. Box 201
Vilhelm Mobergs Gata 4
SE-351 04 Växjö
Sweden

Phone: 46 470 201 20
Fax: 46 470 394 16

E-mail: *info@swemi.se*
Web: *www.swemi.se*

Director: Per Nordahl
Founded: 1965

Description: The Institute is Sweden's national archives and library on emigration. Its purpose is to work for intensified contact between descendants in America of emigrants from Sweden and the country of their ancestors; to develop and further knowledge about the Swedish emigration, especially the emigration to the United States; to establish libraries, archives, and exhibitions for these purposes with material illustrating the history of emigration; and to support scholarly and lay research in this field.

Activities: The Institute collects material on Swedish emigrants and emigration from all over the world. Most of the material, however, relates to the emigration to the United States and Canada. The registers, indexes, and excerpt collections are the largest of their kind with several million computerized register cards. The Institute's library contains Sweden's largest book collection on emigrants and emigration. The House of Emigrants offers a variety of exhibitions open from 9am–4pm on weekdays, 11am–4pm on Saturday. The Institute sponsors lectures, exhibits, and conferences on different topics relating to Swedish emigration. The Institute also acts as a service institution for historians and family researchers with the research room open on weekdays from 9am–4pm.

Publication: Magazine published in June and December, *Emigranten*

Benefits: A book every other year, free entrance to the House of Emigrants, half fee for research on emigrants and relatives.

♛ VOA–Eskilstuna Lodge #633

Hans-Olof Söderström
Eneby 1156 A
SE-635 09 Eskilstuna
Sweden

E-mail: *hans-olof.s@telia.com*

♛ VOA–Småland Lodge #618

Rune Fornander
Resedastigen 9
SE-554 56 Jönköping
Sweden

♛ Wellness of Scandinavia AB

Julie Catterson Lindahl
Vasavägen 24
SE-169 58 Solna
Sweden

Phone: 46 8 82 68 20
Fax: 46 8 82 68 20

E-mail: *julie.catterson@wellnessofscandinavia.com*

Web: *www.wellnessofscandinavia.com*

Chair: Julie Catterson Lindahl

Founded: January 2001

Description: To make known/market a Nordic approach to wellbeing, which includes traditions and lifestyles that can be useful to the health of people anywhere.

Publication: Virtual newsletter for subscribers

Educational Organizations

Academic instruction in Swedish language and culture is offered by a large number of institutions in the United States. Several major universities offer MA and PhD degrees in Scandinavian languages and literature; a number of universities and colleges offer BA degrees in Scandinavian (or Swedish) languages and literature and/or Scandinavian area studies programs.

The list in this section provides an overview of the colleges and universities involved in Swedish studies in one form or another. Also included in this section are the many language programs for families and children.

In addition, a large number of adult education programs at colleges, universities and community colleges offer non-credit courses in the Swedish language. Swedish cultural associations and clubs sometimes offer such courses as well. Sometimes these programs are offered on an irregular or changing schedule. To find out if Swedish language classes are offered, interested individuals should contact local adult education programs or a local Swedish cultural club or association.

👑 *indicates the organization is an affiliate of the Swedish Council of America.*

American Swedish Institute—Svenska Skolan

Nina Clark, Education Programs Coordinator
2600 Park Avenue
Minneapolis, MN 55407

Phone: 612.870.3374
Fax: 612.870.8682

E-mail: *ninac@americanswedishinst.org*
Web: *www.americanswedishinst.org/classes/classes_feb04.htm*

Lead Teacher: Helene Brännström Suh

Founded: 1985

Description: Svenska skolan at ASI is a Saturday morning
Swedish immersion program for children ages 4 and up. The
purpose is to teach children the Swedish language and culture in a challenging and fun environment.

Activities: Classes meet 8 times per session (Fall and Spring) for
3 hours each Saturday.

Benefits: 20% discount shopping day at Christmastime and 2
field trips per year.

Arizona State University

Monika vonEggers
P.O. Box 870202
Tempe, AZ 85287-0202

Phone: 480.965.6281
Fax: 480.965.0135

E-mail: *mvoneggers@asu.edu*
Web: *www.asu.edu/languages/index.htm*

♕ Augustana College

Dr. Larry Scott
Scandinavian Studies
639 38th Street
Rock Island, IL 61201

Phone: 309.794.7655
Fax: 309.794.7443

E-mail: *scscott@augustana.edu*
Web: *www.augustana.edu*

♕ Augustana College

639 38th Street
Rock Island, IL 61201

Phone: 1.800.798.8100 or 309.794.7000

Web: *www.augustana.edu*

President: Steven C. Bahls, **Dean of the College:** Jeff Abernathy

Founded: 1860

Description: Augustana,
  located in Rock Island,
  Illinois, one of several
  cities in the area known
  as the Quad Cities, is an
  independent college of
  the liberal arts and sciences, related to the
  Evangelical Lutheran
  Church in America. The
  college traces its origin
  to the universities of
  Uppsala and Lund in
  Sweden. Graduates of
  these ancient European
  seats of learning founded Augustana in 1860
on the near north side of Chicago.

    Augustana College and Theological Seminary, as it was
first known, moved from Chicago to Paxton, Illinois, in
1863, and finally to Rock Island in 1875. The seminary
became a separate institution in 1948 and in 1967 returned
to Chicago as part of the Lutheran School of Theology.

    Augustana is accredited by the North Central Association of
Colleges and Secondary Schools, the National Association of
Schools of Music, the National Council for the Accreditation
of Teacher Education, and the American Chemical Society.
Since 1948, the college has had a chapter of Phi Beta Kappa.

Concentrated study in a major field within the humanities, the natural or social sciences, or in one of the fields of professional preparation offered at Augustana is required of each student. The college's commitment to the liberal arts is expressed in its general graduation requirements. Each student is asked to study in a broad range of fields, including writing, literature, foreign languages, fine arts, philosophy, religion, social science, natural science, and physical education.

The college's size and character foster personal contact between students and faculty, both inside and outside of formal academic situations. Augustana encourages the personal and academic growth of its students through a full range of co- and extracurricular activities.

The Swedish heritage continues to be identified in many areas of the college's program. Special scholarships are available for students of Swedish descent. A major in Scandinavian offers opportunities for concentrated study of the Swedish language and Scandinavian literature. Majors in Scandinavian, economics, geography, history, or political science may add specialization in Scandinavian Area Studies by taking approved courses in Scandinavian culture. Each year a summer school in Sweden provides the opportunity for intensive language study, and each year students are exchanged with the universities of Uppsala and Karlstad.

Augustana's Thomas Tredway Library holds one of the largest collections of Swedish-American newsprint and periodicals in the United States, and holds what is regarded as the most important collection of manuscripts written by Swedish Lutheran pioneer leaders in America. The archives of the Swenson Swedish Immigration Research Center provide unusually rich opportunities for the study of Swedish-

American history. In addition, the Augustana Historical
Society, which is also associated with the college, preserves
and promotes the heritage and ideas of the Swedish-
Americans who foundeded Augustana Synod and its associated institutions.

The David M. Loring Map Library contains a large number of maps covering the Scandinavian countries. It includes
maps of historic value as well as contemporary culture and
topographic maps.

♕ Bethany College

Scandinavian Studies
421 North First Street
Lindsborg, KS 67456

Phone: 785.277.3311
Fax: 785.227.2004

Web: *www.bethanylb.edu*

Coordinator: McLennan

♛ Bethany College

Bud Rothgeb, Director of Communications and College
  Relations
421 N. First St.
Lindsborg, KS 67456

Phone: 785.227.3311
Fax: 785.227.2004

E-mail: *admission@bethanylb.edu* or *president@bethanylb.edu*
Web: *www.bethanylb.edu*

President: Dr. Paul Formo

Founded: October 15, 1881

Description: Bethany College is a private, four-year, co-educational, liberal arts college dedicated to nurturing and chal-

lenging individuals in their search for truth and meaning as they lead lives of faith, learning and service.

Bethany is a college of the Evangelical Lutheran Church in America (ELCA) and is supported by the Central States, Arkansas–Oklahoma, and Rocky Mountain Synods of the ELCA.

The Rev. Dr. Carl Aaron Swensson, a Lutheran pastor and educator, founded Bethany College in 1881. To this day the College continues to build on the strong heritage passed on by its Swedish Lutheran founders.

Bethany provides a spectrum of academic liberal arts options in a distinctive religious, cultural, and regional setting. Baccalaureate degrees are granted in 14 major areas of study and numerous special programs are offered. Two such special programs are accelerated three-year degree programs in business and economics and a 3+2 engineering program leading to a master's degree in only five years.

The College is renowned for the quality of its education, music, arts, business, social work, pre-professional and pre-engineering programs. It is one of the few places in the Great Plains Region that offers Swedish in its curriculum. The 13 to 1 student faculty ratio ensures personalized attention for all students.

The more than 200-voice Bethany College Oratorio Society has gained regional and national recognition for the quality of its annual Messiah Festival of Music and Art in which Handel's Messiah has been performed at the College during Holy Week for 123 consecutive years. It is the longest running presentation of Handel's Messiah in the United States.

An extensive collection of the paintings and lithographs of the well-known Swedish-American artist and long-time Bethany College faculty member, Birger Sandzén, is located on the campus.

Bethany annually hosts numerous meeting, groups, conferences, sports camps, workshops and cultural events.

Bethany College is accredited by the North Central Association of Colleges and Secondary Schools, the National Association of Schools of Music, the National Council for Accreditation of Teacher Education, and the Council for Social Work Education.

We are proud of our Swedish-American heritage and traditions, which extend back to the earliest immigrant pioneer days of the region, as we look forward to continuing to serve our students, the church and society.

Publications: Magazine, *Bethany Magazine*; Student newspaper, *Bethany Messenger*; Student yearbook, *Bethanian*.

Bethel University

Amanda Wanke
3900 Bethel Dr.
St. Paul, MN 55112

Phone: 651.638.6400 or 800.255.8706
Fax: 651.635.6003

E-mail: *a-wanke@bethel.edu*
Web: *www.bethel.edu*

President: Dr. George Brushaber

Founded: 1871

Description: In 1871, John Alexis Edgren founded a seminary in Chicago for the education of Swedish immigrants. In 1904, Swedish Baptists in Minneapolis started an academy

offering high school-level programs, and the two schools
were brought together on one campus in St. Paul in 1914. In
1931 Bethel Junior College was opened and, subsequent to

the phasing out of the academy, expanded its academic program to become a four-year liberal arts college in 1947. The
seminary relocated to the current campus in Arden Hills in
1965, and the college followed in 1972. Today, the institution is known as Bethel University, which includes the
College of Arts and Sciences, the Graduate School, the
College of Adult and Professional Studies, the School for
Executive Leadership, and Bethel Seminary, which was located in St. Paul, San Diego, and along the East Coast. Bethel
University offers bachelor's degrees in more than 60 majors,
an adult degree completion program, and master's degrees in
several fields of study as well as a doctor of ministry degree
and a doctor of educational administration degree.

Activities: Bethel University maintains its Swedish heritage in many ways, among them the teaching of college courses in Swedish language and culture.

Publications: *Focus, Heart & Mind, Bethel Parent, Royal Investor Newsletter, International Steward, You*

Benefits: Higher education with an evangelical Christian worldview at many points of need: seminary, undergraduate, adult continuing education, and graduate education.

Brigham Young University

Mary Kay Norseng
Scandinavian Studies
SASS, 3003 JKHB
Provo, UT 84602-6118

E-mail: *sass@byu.edu* or *norseng@humnet.ucla.edu*
Web: *www.byu.edu/sasslink*

President: Mary Kay Norseng (University of California)

Founded: 1911

Description: The SASS promotes Scandinavian studies and instruction in America; the encouragement of original research in this country in the fields of Scandinavian languages, literatures, history, culture, and the publication of the results of such research in the quarterly journal, *Scandinavian Studies*; the fostering of closer relations between persons interested in Scandinavian Studies in North America and elsewhere.

Activity: Annual Conference

Publication: Quarterly newsletter, *Scandinavian Studies,*

Benefits: The quarterly newsletter, *Scandinavian Studies, SASS News and Notes*, as well as an open invitation to attend annual meetings and events.

Brown University

Department of German Studies
190 Hope Hall, Box 1979
Providence, RI 02912

Phone: 401.863.2596
Fax: 401.863.9345

Web: *www.brown.edu/Departments/CLS/Languages/Swedish*

California Lutheran University

60 West Olsen Road
Thousand Oaks, CA 91360-2787

Phone: 805.493.3135
Fax: 805.493.3114

E-mail: *cluadm@clunet.edu*
Web: *www.clunet.edu*

President: Luther S. Luedtke, Ph.D.

Founded: 1959

Description: In 1959 the Pederson Ranch, nestled against the rolling hills of Thousand Oaks, began its transformation into the dynamic learning community of California Lutheran University (CLU). Richard Pederson, the son of Scandinavian immigrants, donated his scenic ranch to "provide youth the benefits of a Christian education." The ranch now forms the heart of the expansive 225-acre campus.

Since the first classes were held in 1961, CLU has become a residential university of nearly 3,000 undergraduate and graduate students. The University offers 36 Business and Education as well as master's degrees in business, education, public policy, computer science, and psychology and the Ed.D. in Educational Leadership. Majors in Bioengineering and Environmental Science were added in 2003. Courses are offered at CLU's graduate centers in Ventura and Woodland Hills as well as on the main Thousand Oaks campus.

CLU provides students with a rigorous intellectual experience centered in the liberal arts. As a teaching institution, it places primary emphasis on close relationships between students and faculty who become partners in the learning process. Classes are intentionally kept small.

Major new facilities on campus include Samuelson Chapel, the Soiland Humanities Center, Overton Hall, the Zimmerman Music Studios, the Spies-Bornemann Center for Education and Technology, and Mogen Hall. Projects under construction in 2004 include another 180-student residence hall, a 60 acre sports complex, and a 550-resident continuing care retirement community. Since it went on the

air in 1994, the University's National Public Radio Station,
KCLU, has been recognized as Associate Press Station of the
Year for all California and Nevada. In 1996 CLU received
the nation's highest award for excellence in campus networking.

One of 28 universities affiliated with the Evangelical
Lutheran Church in America (ELCA), CLU is accredited by
the Accrediting Commission for Senior Colleges and
Universities of the Western Association of Schools and
Colleges (WASC) and other specialized bodies. CLU is a
member of the American Council on Education, Council of
Independent Colleges, American Association of Colleges and
Universities, and the Lutheran Educational Conference of
North America.

Many of the founding fathers of the University are of
Swedish descent and numerous Swedish students come to
study at CLU each year. The largest number of CLU's international students are from Scandinavian countries, and the
university has an active exchange program in international
business with the University of Kristianstad.

Activities: CLU's Scandinavian heritage is celebrated in many
ways. Every spring a Scandinavian Festival, one of the largest
and longest running Scandinavian festivals in California,
brings more than 8,000 people to campus to enjoy
Scandinavian food, entertainment, theatrical performances,
art, crafts and lectures. During the Christmas season the
University commemorates the faith and sacrifice of St. Lucia
with a St. Lucia Festival. In conjunction with the
Scandinavian American Cultural and Historical Foundation,
the University houses a Scandinavian Cultural Center on

campus and hosts a major scholarly-cultural conference each year called the Nordic Symposium.

Benefits: Special scholarships are available for students who are of Swedish descent. The Ingeborg Estergren Scholarship provides a year of study in Sweden for a female student majoring in Education. The Victor and Mary Carlson Memorial Scholarship is given to a Swedish or Norwegian senior majoring in History.

Columbia University

Verne Moberg
319 Hamilton Hall
New York, NY 10027

Phone: 212.854.7859
Fax: 212.854.5381

E-mail: *vam1@colombia.edu*
Web: *www.colombia.edu/cu/swedish*

Concordia Language Villages

Christine Schulze
901 S. 8th St
Moorhead, MN 56562

Phone: 1.800.222.4750 or 218.299.4544
Fax: 218.299.3807

E-mail: *clv@cord.edu*
Web: *www.ConcordiaLanguageVillages.org*

Executive Director: Christine Schulze

Founded: 1961

Description: Concordia Language Villages is an internationally recognized and respected world-language and culture-education program, whose mission is to prepare young people for responsible citizenship in our global community. Begun in 1961, the Language Village annually serves 9,500 young people, ages 7–18, from all 50 of the United States, Canada and 24 other countries. CLV has long been a model of quality and innovative programming in immersion education and offers sessions in 13 languages: Chinese, Danish, English, Finnish, French, German, Italian, Japanese, Korean, Norwegian, Russian, Spanish and Swedish. Year-round programs are also available for adults and elderhostelers.

Cornell University

Lena Trancik
Department of German Studies
Goldwin Smitt G71
Ithaca, NY 14853

Phone: 607.255.0702 or 607.254.6574

E-mail: *lgt2@cornell.edu*
Web: *www.people.cornell/edu/pages/lgt2/Swedish*

Föräldraföreningen för Svenskundervisning in New York

Veronica Stolt
515 E. 85th St., Apt. 7C
New York, NY 10028

Phone: 212.628.2867
Fax: 212.472.5917

E-mail: *vstolt@nyc.rr.com*

♛ Gustavus Adolphus College

Department of Scandinavian Studies
800 West College Avenue
St. Peter, MN 56082-1498

Phone: 507.933.7423
Fax: 507.933.7041

Web: *www.gustavus.edu/oncampus/academics/scand-studies*

♛ Gustavus Adolphus College

800 West College Ave.
St. Peter, MN 56082

Phone: 507.933.8000
Fax: 507.933.7081

Web: *www.gustavus.edu*

President: Dr. James L. Peterson

Founded: 1862

Description: Gustavus Adolphus College is a national liberal
arts college affiliated with the Evangelical Lutheran Church
in America. It was founded in 1862 by Eric Norelius in Red
Wing, Minnesota, for the purpose of training pastors and
teachers for Lutheran immigrants from Sweden. The following
year the school was moved to East Union, Carver County,
and given the name of St. Ansgar's Academy. In 1876, it was

again moved, this time to its present location and given the
name Gustavus Adolphus College, after Sweden's king who
died in 1632.

Gustavus Adolphus College is accredited by the North
Central Association of Colleges, the American Chemical
Society, the National Council for the Accreditation of
Teacher Education, and the National League for Nursing. It
also hosts the Eta chapter of Phi Beta Kappa, the nation's
oldest and most prestigious academic honor society, and a
number of other national honor societies.

Gustavus Adolphus College is proud of its Swedish heritage. This pride is manifested through programs and visible memorials that portray Sweden's distinguished contributions to the world in art, science, literature, general culture, and likewise convey the contributions of its Swedish immigrant founders.

Folke Bernadotte Memorial Library, with a capacity of nearly 310,000 volumes and study stations for more than 1,000 students, was dedicated in 1972 by Her Royal Highness Princess Christina. The Bernadotte International Student Scholarship Program has sponsored most of the College's international students since 1950. Another memorial to Count Bernadotte, the Bernodotte Institutes on World Affairs, for 15 years brought world leaders to the campus for discussion of current affairs. The institutes led the College to establish a program in peace education that was hailed as a model in American education.

The Nobel Foundation, Stockholm, has authorized both the Alfred Nobel Hall of Science, dedicated in 1963, and the annual Nobel Conference, which features discussions of science-based issues with Nobel laureates typically among the speakers. The 40th annual Nobel Conference will be held in October 2004, with 6,000 people including scientists, educators, and college and high school students in attendance. The Russell and Rhoda Lund Nobel Endowment, established in 1978, assures a permanent base of support for this respected series.

Activities/Benefits: Four years of Swedish language study are offered along with a strong Scandinavian studies major. Formal exchange programs have been arranged with Växjö University in Småland, Uppsala University, and Mora Folkhögskola.

Each year a number of Swedish students come to study at Gustavus, and there is an active Gustavus alumni chapter based in Stockholm. Gustavus students and faculty regularly participate in a number of study and sabbatical opportunities in Sweden.

The "Out of Scandinavia" program brings leading writers, poets, actors, and other distinguished people in the fine and performing arts and literature to the Gustavus campus through a week-long artist-in-residence program.

Harvard University

James E.Cathey
Herter Hall
Amherst, MA 01003-3925

Phone: 413.545.2350
Fax: 413.545.6995

E-mail: *cathey@german.umass.edu*
Web: *www.umass.edu/germanic/id37.htm*

👑 Jamestown Community College

Moira Lindsley
525 Falconer St.
P.O. Box 20
Jamestown, NY 14701

Phone: 716.665.5220/1.800.388.8557
Fax: 716-665-9110

E-mail: *moiralindsley@mail.sunyjcc.edu*
Web: *www.sunyjcc.edu*

Chairman: L. Durand Peterson, **President:** Dr. Gregory DeCinque

Founded: 1950

Description: Jamestown Community College was founded in 1950 and is one of the thirty public community colleges in New York under the supervision of the State University of New York. JCC offers certificates and associate degrees in a

variety of subjects for both career and transfer students. Approximately half of the students transfer to other colleges and universities after completing their two years at Jamestown Community College. The school is fully accredited and all

credits easily transfer to private and public colleges within
the United States.

Jamestown has a proud history of Swedish immigrants
who account for approximately thirty precent of its population. In an effort to maintain the culture and traditions, a
Scandinavian Studies Program was established at the college
in 1986. The main purpose of the program is to broaden
and strengthen awareness and understanding of the
Scandinavian heritage in the Jamestown community. JCC
works closely with the many Swedish and Scandinavian
groups in the area. A sizable endowment fund was created to
fund programs including student and faculty exchanges.

Kompletterande Svensk Undervisning i Connecticut

Katarina Madden
Scandinavian Club
South Pine Creek Road
Fairfield, CT 06824

Phone: 203.925.3852
Fax: 203.925.3835

E-mail: *kmadden@skandia.com*

Kristinaskolan

P.O. Box 41522
Santa Barbara, CA 93140-1522

Manchester Community College

Harriet Alvord
P.O. Box 1046
Manchester, CT 06046-1046

Phone: 680.512.3000

E-mail: *harriet@discover.net*
Web: *www.mcc.commnet.edu*

Michigan Technical University

Barbara Lide
108 West Calverley Avenue
Houghton, MI 49931-1295

Phone: 906.482.8051
Fax: 906.487.3559

E-mail: *bblide@mtu.edu*
Web: *www.mtu.edu*

♛ Minnehaha Academy

3100 West River Parkway
Minneapolis, MN 55406

Phone: 612.729.8321

Web: *www.minnehahaacademy.net*

President: Dr. John B. Engstrom

Founded: 1913

Description: Minnehaha Academy is owned and operated by
the Northwest Covenant Conference of the Evangelical
Covenant Church of America. The curriculum prepares students for college entrance; in addition, a strong music program and Bibile department are offered. At all campuses and
all age levels, Bible classes and chapel attendance are
required.

Following a decision in 1905 or organize Minnehaha Academy, property was purchased in South Minneapolis near the Mississippi River. The school opened in 1913. The main buliding was erected in 1913. In 1922, an auditorium building was added; in 1949, an auditorium/gymnasium; and in 1977, a fine arts building.

In 1981, a twelve-acre campus, 1.5 miles south of the original campus was purchased. A middle school, grades 6–8, was established there. The upper school remained at the North Campus. In August, 1982, a lower school, grades 1–5, was opened on the South Campus; in 1985, kindergarden was added to the offerings, and in 1995, preschool. In the fall of 1996, a K–5 campus was opened in Bloomington.

In the spring of 2002, a new athletic center was added to the North Campus facilities, freeing up space for the Robert L. Williams Fine Arts Center, the centerpiece of which is the Orville C. Hognander Chapel. This facility was completed in the spring of 2003.

Publication: A quarterly newsletter, *The Arrow*

Minnesota State University–Mankato

Art Department/Scandinavian Studies Program
Nelson Hall 136
Mankato, MN 56001

Phone: 507.389.6412
Fax: 507.389.2816

Web: *www.mnsu.edu/modernlang/scanstudies.html*

New York University

Karin Lundberg
19 University Place
45th Floor
New York, NY 10003-4556

Phone: 212.998.8650
Fax: 212.995.4377

E-mail: *kgo1021@is7.nyu.edu*
Web: *www.nyu.edu/gsas/dept/german*

👑 North Park University

Center for Scandinavian Studies
3225 West Foster Avenue
Chicago, IL 60625-4895

Phone: 773.244.6200

Web: *www.northpark.edu*

♛ North Park University

3225 West Foster Avenue
Chicago, IL 60625-4895

Phone: 773.244.5644

Web: *www.northpark.edu*

President: Dr. David G. Horner; **President and Dean of the Seminary:** Dr. John E. Phelan Jr.; **Academic Dean:** Dr. Charles I. Peterson

Founded: 1891

Description: Located in Chicago, North Park University was founded in 1891 by the Evangelical Covenant Church, a denomination organized by Swedish immigrants. Today,

North Park enrolls more than 2,800 students from around
the globe, providing education through a variety of day,
evening, and weekend programs – from traditional liberal
arts undergraduate education to GOAL, an adult degree
completion program, and master's degrees in business administration, education, management, and nursing. The university, repeatedly ranked as one of "America's Best" by *U.S.
News & World Report*, is accredited by the North Central
Association of Colleges and Secondary Schools. Through
North Park Theological Seminary, the University offers master's degrees in divinity, theology, Christian ministry, and
Christian education, dual degrees with the graduate business
and nursing programs, and a doctor of ministry degree in
preaching.

Approximately 40 transfer students from Scandinavia
study at North Park University. The Norwegian American
Foundation and Sweden-America Foundation assist with the
selection of students from their respective countries. In addition, the Center for Scandinavian Studies (CSS) was chartered in 1984 to foster an understanding between
Scandinavia and America. Exchange programs in Sweden,
Norway, Finland, Iceland, and Denmark administered by the
CSS enable an additional 50 students and several faculty per
year from Scandinavia and United States, providing an excellent opportunity for Scandinavian and American students to
meet.

Guest faculty, artists, and performers from Scandinavia are
invited to the university for classroom and public events,
which also benefit the Scandinavian community in the
Chicago area. Approximately 40 adults are enrolled in the
non-credit Scandinavian language classes to study Swedish,
Norwegian, Danish and Finnish.

A lively interest in the history of Swedish immigrants and in American-Scandinavian cultural relations is evident on campus. The library includes a significant collection of books in Swedish and a special Jenny Lind collection. The campus also houses the archives of the Evangelical Covenant Church as well as the Swedish American Archives of Greater Chicago.

Oglethorpe University–Atlanta

Jay Lutz, PhD
4484 Peachtree Road
Hearst Hall, Room 100
Atlanta, GA 30319

Phone: 404.364.8373

E-mail: *jlutz@facstaff.oglethorpe.edu*

Ohio State University

Department of Germanic Languages and Literatures
320 Cunz Hall, 1841 Millkin Road
Columbus, OH 43210

Phone: 614.292.8687
Fax: 614.292.8510

Web: *www.germanic.ohio-state.edu*

Scandinavian Program–University of Michigan German Department

Johanna Eriksson
812 E. Washington, 3110 MLB
Ann Arbor, MI 48109-1275

Phone: 313.747.0407
Fax: 313.763.6557

E-mail: *johannae@umich.edu*
Web: *www.umich.edu/german/scand.htm*

Director: Johanna Eriksson

Description: The Department of Germanic languages and literatures regularly offers two years of Swedish. Students with special interest and knowledge of Swedish can also enroll for independent studies.

Scandinavian School in San Francisco

Kristina Bünger
Fort Mason Center
San Francisco, CA 94123

Phone: 415.831.9699

E-mail: *info@scandinavianschool.org*
Web: *www.scandinavianschool.org*

Svenska Föräldraföreningen in Charlotte

Ingrid L'Hommedieu
1808 Tanglebriar Court
Weddington, NC 28104

Phone: 704.321.0089

E-mail: *d.lhommedieu@worldnet.att.net*

Svenska Klubben i Montreal

Pernilla Pålsson

E-mail: *pernilla@sprint.ca*
Web: *www.svenskaklubben.just.nu*

Svenska Skolan i Boston

Anna Bark
111 Spiers Road
Newton, MA 02459

E-mail: *info@svenskaskolanboston.org*
Web: *www.svenskaskolanboston.org*

Founded: 1976

Svenska Skolan i Los Angeles

Margaretta Saperston, Rektor
3515 Grandview Blvd.
Los Angeles, CA 90066

Phone: 310.398.5530
Fax: 310.572.6141

E-mail: *svenskaskolanla@yahoo.com*
Web: *www.svenskaskolan.info/la/svenska*

Founded: ca. 1970

Svenska Skolan i New Orleans

Norska Sjömanskyrkan
1772 Prytania Street
New Orleans, LA 70130

Svenska Skolan i Salt Lake City

Terese Whitty
1554 E. Bryan Avenue
Salt Lake City, UT 84105

E-mail: *tmwhitty@uofo.net*

Svenska Skolan i San Diego

Grace Lutheran Church
3993 Park Blvd.
San Diego, CA 92103

Svenska Skolan i Södra Florida

Anette Hallstrand
10322 S.W. 115th Street
Miami, FL 33176

Phone: 305.278.8565
Fax: 305.278.8565

E-mail: *rghred@man.com*

Svenska Skolföreningen i Chicago

Christina Merdinger
407 Harvest Gate
Lake in the Hills, IL 60102

Phone: 847.854.2491

E-mail: *merdingers@att.net*
Web: *www.chapters-swea.org/chicago/sv.skolan.htm*

Svenska Skolföreningen i Michigan

Annika Hjertsson
6853 Granger Drive
Troy, MI 48098-6908

Phone: 810.828.2731
Fax: 810.282.3764

Svenska Skolföreningen i Milwaukee

Annika L. Holm
455 Poplar Creek Drive
Brookfield, WI 53046

Phone: 262.798.9038

E-mail: *aholm@wi.rr.com*

 ## Svenska Skolföreningen i Orange County

Karin Strömberg
555 W. Main St.
P.O. Box B13
Tustin, CA 92781

Phone: 909.509.6844

Web: *www.svenskaskolan.org*

President: Karin Strömberg

Founded: 1996

Description: The goal is to significantly enhance the child's basic understanding of Swedish, through a variety of oral and written activities. As well as to offer each family opportunities to participate in holiday and cultural events throughout the year.

Activities: Easter picnic, Midsummer celebration, Christmas party with Lucia pageant, and a "throwing out the Christmas tree" celebration.

Publication: *Skolnytt*

Svenska Skolföreningen i Philadelphia

Mari Bleacher
1117 Aspen Drive
Narvon, PA 17555

Phone: 717.445.0788
Fax: 717.445.9113

E-mail: *svenskaskolanphiladelphia@yahoo.com*
Web: *www.geocities.com/svenskaskolanphiladelphia*

Svenska Skolföreningen i Phoenix, Inc.

Petra Jacobi
14402 N. 60th Place
Scottsdale, AZ 85254

E-mail: *petrajacobi@msn.com*

Svenska Skolföreningen i Plano

Thomas Moden
4708 White Castle Lane
Plano, TX 75025

E-mail: *tommoden@msn.com*
Web: *www.angelfire.com/tx/swedishschool*

Svenska Skolföreningen i Seattle

Lena Powers
3627 248th Ave. SE
Issaquah, WA 98029

Phone: 425.837.8814

E-mail: *lena@irial.com*
Web: *www.skolforeningen.org*

Svenska Skolföreningen i Silicon Valley, San Jose

Karin Jacobson
Belwood Cabana Club
100 Belwood Gateway
Los Gatos, CA 95032

E-mail: *school@swedschool.org*
Web: *www.swedschool.org*

Svenska Skolföreningen i the Triangle

Anette Nordvall

E-mail: *janette@anettenordvall.com*
Web: *www.anettenordvall.com/Svenskan*

Svenska Skolföreningen i Ventura County

Maria Orange
2110 Upper Ranch Road
Westlake Village, CA 91362

Phone: 805.373.0369
Fax: 805.373.0369

E-mail: *ORANGE1@prodigy.net*
Web: *www.svenskaskolan.info/ventura*

Swedish Educational Association

Gunhild Ljung
32 Hemlock Terrace
Wayne, NJ 07470

Phone: 973.696.2054

E-mail: *gljung@micronav.com*
Web: *www.svenskaskolannj.org*

Swedish Language School of Houston

John Stavinoha
807 Mulberry Ln.
Bellaire, TX 77401-3807

Phone: 713.661.0159
Fax: 713.456.5262

E-mail: *john_stavinoha@mhhs.org*
Web: *www.swedishclub.org/school.htm*

Founded: ca. 1989

Description: The Swedish Club of Houston has maintained a
Swedish Language School for many years. It is the only source
of Swedish language instruction in Southeast Texas. The
school began as a "back porch school" at the home of one of

the Swedish Club's founders and has grown to where it now holds classes at the IKEA store in IH-10 west at Antoine.

As student enrollment demands, the school offers classes at several levels. Instruction is by native speakers of Swedish, and emphasizes a conversational approach since most persons wishing to learn Swedish want to be able to speak it when visiting Sweden.

Benefit: Discount tuition for Swedish Club of Houston members.

Swedish School Association in Sacramento

Christian Olsson
Sacramento, CA

E-mail: *board@swedschoolsac.org*
Web: *www.swedschoolsac.org*

Swedish School Association of Atlanta, Inc.

Christina Allen
4368 Riverview Drive
Duluth, GA 30097

Phone: 770.448.9044
Fax: 770.662.0594

E-mail: *mimms@spritmial.com*

Description: Swedish School has as its objective to teach the Swedish language, culture and traditions to children ages 3–18. Students must have some prior knowledge of Swedish and at least one Swedish parent. All qualified students are welcome regardless of race, color, national or ethnic origin. We meet 10 times per semester, every other Sunday 2–5 P.M. at Mt. Vernon Presbyterian School in Sandy Springs.

Swedish School for Adults

Margareta Storm
9505 Mandolin Court
Vienna, VA 22182

Phone: 703.938.3549

E-mail: *mstorm9505@aol.com*

Description: For adults who want to study Swedish as a foreign language. Meets at George Mason Jr./Sr. High School, Falls Church, VA

Swedish School for Children, Inc.

Lena Lake
13062 Pershing Drive
Manassas, VA 20112

Phone: 703.791.0246

E-mail: *svenskabarn@verison.net*
Web: *www.svenskabarn.com*

Founded: 1972

Description: In operation since 1972, the Swedish School is supported financially by the Swedish government, student tuition, and private contributions. The school is open to children between the ages of 5 and 18 and meets every Saturday morning from 9:30 a.m. to noon during the regular school year (from the beginning of September to the first week in June). The Swedish School for Children draws students from throughout the greater Washington area.

Activities: Apart from the more traditional classroom instruction, the Swedish School for Children offers many other activities and opportunities: an exciting Christmas Party with a Lucia pageant, lottery, lussekatter and pepparkakor; an Easter Open House with arts and crafts, semlor and a Swedish book table; an End-of-School-Year Picnic; a library with Swedish books, cassettes, and videos; music with a music teacher who teaches Swedish songs and rhymes.

♛ Swedish School in Marin

Eva Carlston-DeWolfe
P.O. Box 144
Ross, CA 94957

Phone: 415.454.2878
Fax: 415.454.2922

E-mail: *evadewolfe@comcast.net*

President: Eva DeWolfe

Founded: January, 2000

Description: Teaching children between the ages of 3 and 12 years old the Swedish language, culture and traditions.

Activities: We celebrate Lucia, Christmas, Påsk, Semmeldagen and Midsommar

Swedish School in Portland

Herje Wikegård
Friendly House
1737 N.W. 26th Ave.
Portland, OR 97210

Phone: 503.228.4391

E-mail: *persson_nilla@hotmail.com*
Web: *www.swedishschool.org*

Tennessee Foreign Language Institute

404 James Robertson Pkwy.
Suite 1510
Nashville, TN 37219

Phone: 615.741.7579
Fax: 615.741.7331

Founded: 1986

Description: The Tennessee Foreign Language Institute provides foreign language classes for anyone with a desire to learn about another culture. We offer classes year-round and welcome anyone desiring a fun and effective language learning experience. We offer everything from Arabic to Swedish to Vietnamese. Our classes are small to provide as much one-on-one interaction with our instructors as possible. We focus more on the communicative aspect of learning the language. We believe that being able to communicate in a foreign language is the key to connecting people from all parts of the globe.

Tre Kronor—Svenska Skolföreningen i San Francisco Bay Area

Ami Rådström-Ditzel
5550 Merritt Drive
Concord, CA 94521

Phone: 925.672.2322

E-mail: *tre_kronor_san_francisco@hotmail.com*

University of Alberta

Marianne Lindvall
Dept. of Modern Languages and Comparative Studies
300 Arts
Edmonton, AB
T6G 2E6

Phone: 780.492.4144
Fax: 780.492.9112

E-mail: *lindvall@ualberta.ca*
Web: *www.arts.ualberta.ca/~scand*

University of British Columbia

Lena Karlström
Dept. of German Studies
1873 East Mall
Vancouver, BC
V6T 1Z1

Phone: 604.822.6403
Fax: 604.822.9344

E-mail: *lenak@interchange.ubc.ca*
Web: *www.german.ubc.ca*

University of California–Berkeley

Department for Scandinavian Studies
6303 Dwinelle Hall #2690, University of California
Berkeley, CA 94720-2690

Phone: 510.642.4484
Fax: 510.642.6220

Web: *http://ls.berkeley.edu/dept/scandinvian*

University of California–Los Angeles

The Scandinavian Section, UCLA
212 Royce Hall, Box 951537
Los Angeles, CA 90095-1537

Phone: 310.825.6828
Fax: 310.825.9754

Web: *www.humnet.ucla.edu/humnet/scandinavian/index.html*

University of Cincinnati

730-742 Old Chemistry Building
Mail Location #372
Cincinnati, OH 45221-0372

Phone: 513.556.2755
Fax: 513.556.1991

Web: *asweb.artsci.uc.edu/german/swe2.html*

University of Colorado–Boulder

Eva Tadell
Germanic and Slavic Languages and Literatures
Campus Box 276
Boulder, CO 80309-0276

Phone: 303.492.8827
Fax: 303.492.5376

Web: *www.colorado.edu*

University of Illinois–Urbana/Champaign

Department of Germanic Languages and Literatures
707 South Mathews Avenue
Urbana, IL 61801-3675

Phone: 217.333.1288
Fax: 217.244.3242

Web: *www.germanic.uiuc.edu/ebbaalm/svenskasidor/svframe*

University of Maryland–College Park

Rose-Marie G. Oster
3215 Jimenez Hall
College Park, MD 20742

Phone: 301.405.4096
Fax: 304.314.9841

E-mail: *ro8@umail.umd.edu*
Web: *www.umd.edu*

University of Massachusetts

Scandinavian Studies

Phone: 413.545.2350
Fax: 413.545.6995

E-mail: *cathey@german.umass.edu*
Web: *www.umass.edu/germanic/id37.htm*

Staff: James E. Cathey

 University of Michigan–Ann Arbor

Johanna Ericksson
812 East Washington Street
Ann Arbor, MI 48109-1295

Phone: 313.747.0407
Fax: 313.763.6557

E-mail: *johannae@umich.edu*
Web: *222.lsa.umich.edu/german/scand.htm*

♕ University of Minnesota: Center for Scandinavian Studies

Monika Zagar
230 Folwell Hall
9 Pleasant St. SE
Minneapolis, MN 55455

Phone: 612.625.3388
Fax: 612.624.8287

E-mail: *scan@umn.edu*
Web: *www.cla.umn.edu/scanctr*

Director: Monika Zagar

Description: The mission of the Center of Scandinavian Studies is to advance teaching and research of Scandinavian languages, societies and cultures by sharing researched, based and other forms of knowledge across disciplines; fostering research and action projects; serving as a focal point for Scandinavian Studies at the University of Minnesota and in North America.

University of Oregon

Department of Germanic Languages and Literatures
202 Friendly Hall, 1250 University of Oregon
Eugene, OR 97403-1250

Phone: 503.346.4051
Fax: 503.346.4126

Web: *www.uoregon.edu/~uopubs/bulletin/CAS/scandinavia_*

University of Pennsylvania–Philadelphia

Kim-Eric Williams
745 Williams Hall
Philadelphia, PA 19104-6305

Phone: 215.898.7332
Fax: 215.573.7794

E-mail: *kimeric@sas.upenn.edu*
Web: *ccat.sas.upenn.edu/german/swedish.html*

University of Southern Mississippi Center for Oral History and Cultural Heritage

Box 5175
Hattiesburg, MS 39406-5175

Phone: 601.266.4574
Fax: 601.266.6357

E-mail: *charles.bolton@usm.edu*
Web: *www.usm.edu/oralhistory*

Co-Directors: Charles Bolton and Curtis Austin

Description: The Oral History Program collects interviews on a wide variety of topics relating to Mississippi History and culture. The Program also helps to promote the collection of oral histories through outreach programs such as the Mississippi Oral History Program (a joint project with the Mississippi Humanities Council) and a radio series featuring examples from the Center's collection.

Activities: Ethnic Groups in Mississippi 1971–1982: 33 taped interviews with members of ethnic groups living in Mississippi, including Chinese, Finnish, French, Greek, Italian, Lebanese, Slavic, Swedish and Vietnamese.

University of Texas–Austin

Lynn Wilkinson
Department of Germanic Studies
Campus Mail Code C3300, E.P. Schoch 3.102
Austin, TX 78712-1190

Phone: 512.471.4123
Fax: 512.471.4025

E-mail: *lrw@mail.utexas.edu*
Web: *www.utexas.edu/depts/germain/main.html*

♛ University of Washington, Department of Scandinavian Studies

Terje Leiren
318 Raitt Hall
Box 353420
Seattle, WA 98195-3420

Phone: 206.543.0645
Fax: 206.685.9173

E-mail: *uwscand@u.washington.edu*
Web: *http://depts.washington.edu/scan*

Department Chair: Terje I. Leiren

Founded: 1909

Description: Established in 1909 by an act of the Washington State Legislature, the Department of Scandinavian Studies offers courses of study in the language, literature, history, politics, folklore and cultures of the five Scandinavian (Nordic) countries.

Publication: Department newsletter

♛ University of Wisconsin–Madison

Susan Brantly
Department of Scandinavian Studies
1306 Van Hise Hall, 1220 Linden Drive
Madison, WI 53706

Phone: 608.262.9637
Fax: 608.262.9417

E-mail: *sbrantly@facstaff.wisc.edu*
Web: *www.scandinavian.wisc.edu*

Chair: Susan Brantly

Founded: 1875

Description: Offering undergraduate and graduate degrees in
Scandinavian Studies.

Activities: A number of guest lectures each year and a weekly
Swedish conversation table.

Publication: Annual newsletter.

University of Wisconsin–Milwaukee

Department of Foreign Languages and Linguistics
P.O. Box 413
Curtin Hall 829
2143 N. Downer Avenue
Milwaukee, WI 53201-0413

Phone: 414.229.4948
Fax: 414.229.2741

E-mail: *mam@csd.uwm.edu*
Web: *www.uwm.edu/dept/fll*

Vassar College

Gunilla Feroe
P.O. Box 0269
Chicago Hall 121, 124 Raymond Avenue
Poughkeepsie, NY 12604

Phone: 845.437.5729

E-mail: *guferoe@vassar.edu*
Web: *http://silp.vassar.edu/swedish.html*

Resources

The Swedish-American press, generally in failing health for a number of years, has shown signs of renewal. Modernization and marketing by a new generation of owners, together with new publications, has reversed declining circulation. This section includes the predominant newspapers and periodicals available in North America.

In addition to these predominant newspapers, many organizations publish newsletters for their members and are circulated regionally or nationally. These publications are listed under each of the independent organizations.

The advent of the Internet has opened new avenues of information. It provides access to news in Sweden as soon as it is available there. For information about Sweden, *www.sweden.se* serves as the nation's official Internet gateway. The site is administered by the Swedish Institute and is a cooperative effort by the Swedish Government Offices, Swedish Trade Council, Invest in Sweden Agency, Swedish Travel & Tourism Council, and Swedish Institute. The availability of Swedish American information continues to expand as more organizations and publications develop home pages. These Internet sites are listed under each of the independent organizations.

 indicates the resource is an affiliate of theSwedish Council of America.

Bryggan—The Bridge

Rod Johnston
301 Norwood Dr.
Georgetown, TX 78628

E-mail: *tommy@hellstrom.net*
Web: *www.emigrantregistret.s.se/BRIDGE.htm*

President: Tommy Hellstrom

Description: Encourages research concerning emigration on
both sides of the Atlantic Ocean. A good picture of what is
happening in research at different levels is reviewed. The
activities of various Swedish-American organizations is also
covered.

California Veckoblad—Swedish American Newspaper Company

Jane Hendricks
10921 Paramount Blvd.
Downey, CA 90241

Phone: 562.646.3373
Fax: 562.862.4880

E-mail: *janehendricks@juno.com*

Editor: Jane Hendricks, **Owner:** Mary Hendricks

Founded: 1910

Publication: Eight standard size pages, printed twice a month, with three pages in Swedish. Approximately: $20 a month.

Svenska Amerikanaren Tribunen—The Swedish American Newspaper

10921 Paramount Blvd.
Downey, CA 90241

Editor: Jane Hendricks

Founded: 1876

Publication: Twelve standard size pages, twice a month. Two to three pages in Swedish.

Subscription: $25 per year

♛ Swedish News (2 publications)

P.O. Box 1710
New Canaan, CT 06840

Phone: 203.299.0380 or 1.800.827.9333
Fax: 203.299.0381

Editor & Publisher: Ulf E. Mårtensson

Nordic Reach

E-mail: *info@nordicreach.com*
Web: *www.nordicreach.com*

Founded: 2000

Description: *Nordic Reach* is all about combining the best of Scandinavia and America; it is for people with a taste for Scandinavian culture, design, lifestyles and perspectives.

Publication: Quarterly: February, June, September & November

Nordstjernan

E-mail: *info@nordstjernan.com*
Web: *www.nordstjernan.com*

Founded: 1872

Description: Each week for 130+ years, *Nordstjernan* has provided its loyal readership with pertinent news from Sweden and the US in a unique mix of business, financial, commercial, political, sports and current event coverage. To make the weekly summary of significant events and trends a reality, Nordstjernan publishes transmissions for more than a dozen correspondents and reporters-at-large spanning North America and Sweden. In addition, our one-of-a-kind columnists deliver new insights into Sweden and international affairs, all from a Swedish perspective. Our content is 80% in English, 20% in Swedish.

Publication: Weekly

♛ Swedish Press Society (2 publications)

Anders Neumueller
1294 W 7th Avenue
Vancouver, BC
V6H 1B6

Phone: 604.731.6381
Fax: 604.731.2292

E-mail: *office@nordicway.com*
Web: *www.nordicway.com*

Editor: Anders Neumueller

Founded: 1929

Scandinavian Press

Founded: Autumn of 1994

Description: *Scandinavian Press* brings you the old traditions as well as the latest trends, lifestyles, arts, sports and business. You meet famous Scandinavians like Thor Heyerdahl and Queen Margrethe of Denmark in exclusive interviews. A family invites you over to share their best receipes and a calendar keeps you informed about events. You can get *Scandinavian Press* by subscription or through newsdealers in all of North America.

Swedish Press

Founded: 1929

Description: The Society was formed to secure the continued publication of *Swedish Press—Nya Svenska Pressen*.

Publication: *Swedish Press—Nya Svenska Pressen*, a monthly magazine.

The Sun: Scandinavian–USA News

1780 Copper Lane
Evergreen, CO 80439-9406

Phone: 303.670.6578
Fax: 303.670.8627

E-mail: *scansun@worldnet.att.net*

President: Karen Johnson Gagen

Founded: 1992

Description: Monthly newspaper/magazine in English, distributed through Canada and the USA. It is filled with news and information in sections for each nationality in Scandinavia as well as business and international interests. There are twenty plus tabloid pages.

    Also includes: event calendars, lifestyles, and feature stories.

Publication: Monthly ($20 per year)

Vestkusten

237 Ricardo Road
Mill Valley, CA 94941

Phone: 415.381.5149
Fax: 415.381.9664

E-mail: *info@vestkusten.com*
Web: *www.vestkusten.com*

President: Barbro Sachs-Osher

Founded: 1886

Description: *Vestkusten* is one of the oldest Swedish American newspapers that keep readers updated in both English and Swedish with news from Sweden—politics, events, business and sports—and with the people, organizations and events in the active Swedish-American community in the West.

Publication: Semi-monthly

Geographical
Index

United States

Alaska

Anchorage

Alabama

Thorsby

Arizona

Mesa

Phoenix

Prescott Valley

Scottsdale

Colorado

Delaware

Florida

Kansas

Wichita

Kentucky

Florence

Lexington

Louisiana

New Orleans

Maine

Maryland

Massachusetts

Michigan

Mississippi

Missouri

Montana

Nebraska

New Hampshire

New Jersey

New Mexico

New York

Baldwin

Bronx, New York City

Brooklyn, New York City

Buffalo

Endicott

Freeport

Glenville

Puerto Rico

Rhode Island

Tennessee

Texas

Virgin Islands

Virginia

Washington DC

Washington

Anacortes

Bothell

Everett

Issaquah

Kirkland

Longview

Ocean Park

Canada

Alberta

British Columbia

Manitoba

New Brunswick

Fredericton

Nova Scotia

Dartmouth

Halifax

Ontario

Ottawa

Thunder Bay

Sweden

Sunne

Växjö

Alphabetical
Index

1- 4/05